Living in God's Army: Instructions from a Warrior of David

Rabbi Moshe Laurie

With
Mary Elliott
And
Martha Laurie, Ph.D.

Living in God's Army: Instructions from a Warrior of David
by Rabbi Moshe Laurie

Printed in the United States of America

ISBN 9781626971967

www.xulonpress.com

Acknowledgements

*B*aruch Ata Adoni! Blessed are You, O Lord! Above all, we acknowledge that it is only because of the Lord that this book was completed. It is with His protection and supernatural healing over the 18 months before this book went to press that we were able to complete this work.

We thank Antonia for photography, photo editing and graphics and Angie for photo editing. We are grateful that Donna listened to the prompting of the Holy Spirit and traveled a great distance to be with us at a time of great need. Finally, to Congregation Adat Ariel, ShofarBeTzion Ministries and all our friends around the country and around the world who have been covering us in prayer — May God bless you abundantly!

Foreword

*W*hy is this book different from any other book on spiritual warfare? My husband, Rabbi Moshe Laurie, is different from any other Messianic Rabbi. It's not that he hosted his own Christian television program from 2004 until 2009. The first twelve shows were based on a class that he had previously taught many times, "Spiritual Warfare: Joining God's Army." The popularity of his program was due to his unique perspective. Just as the New Testament rests on the foundation of the Hebrew Tanach, known to most Christians as the Old Testament, spiritual warfare has Hebrew roots. He learned this foundation through his studies at Yeshiva as an adult.

He was a warrior in the flesh, first serving in the US Marine Corps. He went on to serve Israel in undercover operations, became an Israeli citizen, and then served in drug interdiction for the National Police and in the Israel Defense Forces as assistant commander of the Sniper School. He was thirty-nine years old when the Lord spoke to him audibly, and he recognized that his Jewish Messiah was Jesus. When he asked the Lord what to do now, he received the word, "The disciplines of the flesh shall be the disciplines of the spirit. Dare in my name as I show you."

Many television—and now radio—viewers have written personal letters to Rabbi Moshe expressing their gratitude and warm wishes. He is a friend to those who know him as well as those who have never met him in person. His personality is exactly the same on the air and off; he is forceful, warm, funny, outgoing, outspoken and often exuberant. He is biblically correct and politically incorrect. His presentation is casual. You might say that you can take the boy out of Brooklyn, but you can't take Brooklyn out of the boy. I certainly wouldn't want to change him. The challenge in helping him with this book was to create a readable text that reflects his personal teaching style and his unique insights.

The reader may notice that this book is short and is divided into short chapters. It should be read from beginning to end, because later chapters build upon concepts that have already been introduced. However, when the Rabbi teaches, he reviews, questions and interacts with students. In his television programs, he used this same teaching style. We encourage the reader to be actively engaged, looking up the Scriptures in your Bible and asking the Lord to speak to you through these teachings. As in the Bible, if something in this book is restated two or three times, pay attention. Finally, although this book will strengthen new believers, all believers who regularly check their spiritual armor will be excited to learn the Old Testament foundations of spiritual warfare.

We will know we have succeeded if "Living in God's Army: Instructions from a Warrior of David" becomes a book that you find encouraging, uplifting and empowering when you are under attack. As the Rabbi says,

Chazak Ve Amatz Em Chochma
(Strong and Courageous with Wisdom)

Martha Laurie

Table of Contents

Chapter 1 What I Believe.. 9
Chapter 2 What Do You Believe? 11
Chapter 3 Choose and Choice 17
Chapter 4 Commit to Obey 21
Chapter 5 Hear and Do.. 25
Chapter 6 Obey, Submit, Be Humble.............................. 29
Chapter 7 Come As a Child 35
Chapter 8 Forgive 39
Chapter 9 Practice.. 41
Chapter 10 Warriors in Training 43
Chapter 11 Stand Before the Lord..................................... 47
Chapter 12 The Armies of God 51
Chapter 13 Release of the Warriors 55
Chapter 14 Empowered 61
Chapter 15 Joining God's Army... 67
Chapter 16 Understanding Who You Are.......................... 71
Chapter 17 Your Position as a Warrior.............................. 77
Chapter 18 Protected Under the Hand of God 83
Chapter 19 A Weapon for Today....................................... 89
Chapter 20 The Spiritual War 93

Chapter 1

WHAT I BELIEVE

S halom. My name is Rabbi Moshe Laurie and we will be taking a look at "Living in God's Army." Why should you even bother reading this book? It is about spiritual warfare, but not about anything that is different from what you should be doing every day. If you are a believer in Jesus, the Son of God, by whatever name you call Him, you are in God's Army. You will be attacked by satan, whether you like it or not. You are wise to be well trained, so that you will be strengthened and empowered. Rejoice! You have nothing to fear.

Who am I that I can tell you these things? Well, personally I'm nobody very special, except that I started as an Orthodox Jew born in Williamsburg, Brooklyn, New York. From the age of nine years old I wanted to become a Warrior of David. I lived most of my adult life as an Orthodox Jew working with the Israeli government in various capacities. I traveled the world helping hunt the enemies of Israel as I lived undercover for over twenty years under assumed names. It was wonderful — or so I thought.

Then I had a supernatural experience, as I went from being a Zionist-Nationalist Christian-hater, to a Zionist-Nationalist believer in the one true living God through the Messiah that I know as Yeshua, the Hebrew name for Jesus. I was living in Israel when I accepted Jesus and declared, "The Messiah's come and His name is Jesus!" I was divorced against my will, lost my children and my job, and they cancelled my passport. I'm surprised I wasn't killed.

The issue is that this was the choosing that I made. I could have denounced the Messiah, said I was crazy and left Christianity. I could have come home, sat with the rabbi for six months and then said, "Listen, due to the stress of my job, I went a little crazy. This guy Jesus, well he is just a prophet. I'm sorry."

I couldn't do that because I did believe. I'm a Jew who believes in Jesus. I'm a Messianic. (Messianic as in the word "Messiah.") Rabbi. I'm a Messianic Rabbi who leads a Messianic congregation. We believe in the Father, the Son, and the Holy Spirit. We believe in the Messiah—Jesus, whose name in Hebrew before it was translated into Jesus was Yeshua. Yeshua is what His mother called Him.

Messianic believers worship on the Sabbath—Friday evening and Saturday, but I do visit churches on Sunday. The only difference between our Jewish brethren and us is we've already received the Messiah and the law does not bind us. All Jews are supposed to be Messianic, but many are waiting for the Messiah to come for the first time. The issue is that I am a Messianic Jewish believer; there are Messianic believers who are not Jewish by birth. As long as you believe in the Father, the Son and the Holy Spirit, the accuracy of the Bible, and the Messiah and His coming—then we are on the same ground and we are believers of like faith.

We (Jews who believe in Jesus) are waiting for the Messiah to come the second time. There are more and more of us (Messianic Jews) around the world, but let's not be concerned whether I'm a Messianic Jew or a Christian, I just want you to know that hopefully we are all of like mind and like faith. We study the same Bible from Genesis to Revelation. We believe in the same Father, Son and Holy Spirit. We believe in the same Trinity and Holy Ghost power of God. If you don't want to believe that, I encourage you to continue reading.

When I began teaching, I would not include new believers in the class, but I have begun to feel this is so important that all who would hear should know. Once you know what you are going to learn here, it becomes an obligation. You may be blissfully ignorant (and I'm not calling anybody ignorant), but you may be blissfully ignorant because you think if you don't know something you're not held accountable. Seek God and ask Him whether you need more of what you will be reading in this book.

Chapter 2

WHAT DO YOU BELIEVE?

O ne of the things I discovered when I became a new believer is that there was such a thing as a burned-out Christian. I found this to be difficult as I was one who had believed in the Bible all my life. A Jew starts studying the Torah (the first five books of the Bible) at the age of five. You don't learn very much at such a young age, but you still begin at the age of five to study the Hebrew language. You learn your morning prayers, your afternoon prayers and through your childhood into adulthood you're taught that the Lord God is the foundation of all things. You learn how to greet God, how to recognize God, how to become "God aware." So here I come, taking the Bible as absolute fact from Genesis to the end of the Old Testament.

Then one day the Lord speaks to me audibly, saying that the Messiah is Jesus! "You can serve the Father through Me; you will serve the Father through Me, for I have come in his stead." It was a supernatural experience. It changed my life! Terrible things happened in the beginning. I was divorced against my will, my children were taken away, my Israeli passport was cancelled and my family had a funeral! Nobody talked to me for a very, very long time. All kinds of great and terrible things happened, but since then the Lord has returned that which the cankerworm has stolen. (Joel 2:25)

When I received the Messiah and became a brand new believer, I had to learn what is called the "New Testament," so I read it. The Christian Bible starts in the book of Genesis and ends with the book of Revelation. The Hebrew Bible, the Tanach, includes the books from Genesis to Malachi. It reads the Hebrew way, from back to front and from right to left. The only difference between these two books is the Holy Bible is the complete Bible. For thirty-nine years I didn't know that complete Bible. In that complete Bible I found answers to questions like "Who are 'Us?'"

Genesis 1:26 says, "And God said, 'Let Us make Man in our own image. . .'" Nobody knew who the "Us" was. Now I know "Us" is the Father, Son and Holy Spirit. Just don't ask an unsaved Jew because he'll tell you that if God wants to call himself "Us" who are we to question Him? I read things like the nine gifts of the Spirit (First Corinthians 12: 8-10) and the infilling of the Holy Spirit (Acts 2). I read things about healing; I read things about the many promises of God. This is what we're going to be looking at throughout this book—how to receive the foundations of spiritual warfare.

What did I discover about spiritual warfare? I asked the Lord, "Why are things happening? Why are Christians that were founded—they weren't making mistakes— they weren't in sin— they weren't doing the terrible, horrible things that God told them not to do. . .why are things happening to them?" One of the things that the Lord showed me was to look at what I had done most of my life. How could I go undercover for many of these years and not burn out? Now it wasn't fun and it was a lot of stress. The only time I used my own name was when I went back to the homeland to be with my wife and two children at that time.

I started noticing that most believers do spiritual warfare like sports, not that they take it lightly. But how does a professional athlete or any athlete who does a sport regularly train? He learns the sport and he does it the best he can. For example, I'm a fencer so I learned the basics of fencing. I learned advanced fencing and then got to the point in my training where I was competent enough to compete. Ok, so what did I do? I would practice, practice, practice, and then when it was time for competition I would begin to ramp up my training. Just at the day of the competition, hopefully I had timed the training right so I would peak.

I would be at my best level of competence and what would happen then? Hopefully I'd win, by being the best of the best because I timed it correctly. Then I'd ramp back down to a mainte-nance level of training so I could keep the proficiency, but I wasn't capable of remaining at that high level of training. I want you to remember this because I'm going to show you that you cannot – you cannot – do spiritual warfare with a constant high level of training. It is physically impossible to maintain a high level artificially and this is why people are burning out.

Now why do we have problems, and why are we supposed to do spiritual warfare in the first place? What is spiritual warfare? Where did it come from? The Lord didn't leave things to chance. He wrote the Bible through His people and He wrote it supernaturally. As far as I'm concerned every Word in the Bible is accurate, and if we keep it simple, every Word is exactly as written and no other way. God made the Bible simple. Yes is yes and no is no. The Lord told us very carefully what we're supposed to do, and what we're not supposed to do.

Let's take a look at Genesis 1:26-28. The Tanach states (translated from Hebrew), "And God said, 'Let us make Man in Our image, after Our likeness. They shall rule over the fish of the sea, the birds of the sky, and over the animal, the whole earth, and every creeping thing that creeps upon the earth.' So God created Man in His image, in the image of God He created him; male and female He created them. God blessed them and God said to them, 'Be fruitful and multiply, fill the earth and subdue it; and rule over ('have dominion' – KJV) the fish of the sea, the bird of the sky, and every living thing that moves upon the earth.'" By the by, that's just about everything isn't it?

What does it mean to rule over – to have "dominion over?" To have "dominion over" is to have ultimate control over everything going on above and below this earth. Now we are getting to the basic foundational principles. We need to go through this because there are some people who have never bothered to look at this or didn't think it was important. But you see God gave the devil dominion over the earth. Is that not true? Can anyone disagree here? No. God gave the devil dominion over the earth. ". . .your adversary the devil, as a roaring lion, walketh about, seeking whom he may devour" (First Peter 5:8). We as believers do not have to give the devil permission. The Lord commands us to take dominion and subdue (Genesis 1:28). That means that the devil has dominion over the earth and everything except that which the believer – you and I – take back.

Now in order to do this, we have to know who we are. We have to know what we're going to be doing, and we have to know how to do it. We get back to the very basics on how you join God's army. First you have to accept certain premises. You have to ask yourself — do I believe that God is God? Now you say, "He's going back to the beginning, I know better than that!" The question is — do you know that this is what you need to know? Not that God is some God way over there, but that the Lord is God here, and that He created the heaven and the earth and that He created it for today. He created everything — us, the earth and all the things He has given us dominion over. Do you believe that?

Do you believe that the Bible as written is the supernatural instruction manual that was given for us? Do you believe it? If you don't, then this book is not for you. Seek out a church and ask a pastor these questions. You need to find a true believer in the Lord because you need to know that God is God, that He created the heaven and the earth, and that the Bible is accurate in every Word. We need an understanding that God is a big enough God to make it so. If we ask him and desire — this is the keyword — and desire that we be enabled to do that which He has commanded, then God will make it so!

Now ask yourself if you believe that there is a Messiah? Is his Hebrew name Yeshua, which we translate as Jesus? Did He come? Did He come in the supernatural virgin birth? Did He die and then rise? Did he live on this earth as a child? Did He live on earth as an adult? Did He walk as a man? Did He see the infilling of the Holy Spirit? Did He receive it? What on earth does this have to do with spiritual warfare? If you can't put on the weapon — if you don't understand the weapon — you can't use it! You need to know who God is, the Bible is accurate and Jesus is the Messiah. Receive it! You need to know that He died and rose again and now sits at the right hand of God and that there is a Holy Spirit and He is released into us. You need to accept these things.

I used to think that without the Holy Spirit you had a car without a supercharger. But no, it's way worse than that! What you have is a car running on three cylinders when it should run on eight. The car is working, you have the power, you have the ability, you have the gas, you have everything going; but if you do not have the Father, the Son and the Holy Spirit and you do not understand the instruction manual, then you're driving on way less power than you could be. Let's assume that if you have not asked the Messiah to come into your heart, that you will do so now. Ask the Lord to come be your Lord, to come be your Savior, and ask Him to clarify and show you what the Bible is.

Ask the Lord to infill you — please come Holy Spirit! It's that simple! When I became a believer, I knew nothing about Christianity because I was raised in Judaism. People told me to receive the Holy Spirit and I asked them "How?" Then they would tell me how to receive it and I would run around and try. I drove people crazy for about two days, and then I watched someone else receiving the Holy Spirit. I put out my hand to pray for them and the Holy Spirit came. If your heart's desire is to have what God has for you, He will make the way.

If you believe that God is God, the Lord is the Messiah, the Bible is accurate as written, and the Holy Spirit has returned as our intercessor and attorney, then you have the foundation to begin. You have to ask yourself if you really want to know these things, because if you don't know them, you may be able to get away with not being jumped on right now. If you're looking for highly technical terms and subject matter, this is the wrong book to read. Ask yourself if you're willing to accept the responsibility. If not, you have to stop reading this right now because if you don't you will be obligated — not to me — but to God.

Chapter 3

CHOOSE AND CHOICE

A dam and Eve got kicked out of the Garden of Eden. How did that happen? Realize that the Lord has given us the ability to freely choose. Not a free choice — that is a lie of the devil! It's a word that was stolen. In order to receive all that you can, you have to "choose." Choice is not something you do. Choice is not something you make. It's something you get when you choose correctly.

I have a reproduction — an exact copy — of Noah Webster's English dictionary originally published in 1828. It is filled with Scriptures illustrating the meaning of words. In the Bible the King James Version has twenty Scriptures in the Old Testament that contain the word "choice." Not one verse speaks about making a "choice." When you go to a butcher and ask for the best cut of meat, you ask for the "choice cut." You can look up these Scriptures with your concordance or a free on-line Bible program. You will be amazed to find the "choice and mighty men of valor." (1 Chronicles 7:40) It talks about the "choice cedars of Lebanon." (Ezekiel 31:16) Even when one came to buy the sepulcher (a grave), the prince commands the people to show them the "choice sepulchers." (Genesis 23:6)

In more recent editions the editors eliminated the Scriptures and changed the meanings of words. Pay close attention to what I'm telling you. We've been told in the newer editions of the dictionary and in our societal teachings that everyone has free choice. Humanists have taken over our educational systems since the mid to late 1800's and made changes to our vocabulary. In the copy of Webster's original dictionary, the meaning of marriage is three and a half columns long and over two pages, including all related Scriptures. Even if you take the Scriptures out, the definition of marriage is at least two whole columns! When I was first given the Webster's dictionary as a gift, I taught out of it. You can teach out of it because it is based on the Bible.

Humanism tries to teach us that we have freedom and you do have the freedom! God has given you the freedom, but Humanists don't want to give God the credit. If you choose correctly — and the only way you can choose correctly is God — you get "the choice" — "the best." If you choose incorrectly, you get the "not so good" or "really bad." Humanism tries to tell you that no matter what you choose, it is OK. . .feel good. . .do what you're told. . .do what you want. . .do what they tell you, but it means you're supposed to do what you're told. That's why they call the abortion murderers "pro-choice." It implies that they can choose whatever they want and get what is best for them. They get the choice — the choice of murder. That's the only choice they're really making.

Try for the next two or three days to take the word "choice" out of your vocabulary. Whenever you talk about making a decision, it will sound different because you've been trained to say I'm making a choice to do this. Try to say instead, "I am choosing to do this" and "I choose to obey God," because there is a right and a wrong. Humanists and the satanists and all of these "ist's" are trying to take right and wrong away from us. They're trying to take away our moral foundation, but the right choosing is God. The right choosing is the Word of God and choosing correctly is what the Lord says to do. If we act according to the Word of God, we will receive the "choice."

I was raised in Judaism; there were many things when I became a new believer in Christ that made absolutely no sense whatsoever. The reason I was able to do them is because of what we Jews have been taught since the very beginning of our education. If "God said so," then that's the reason you do it. How many times did you ask your parents, "Why should I do this?" We learned to accept "Because I said so!" There are many reasons, but the foundational reason that you should do something is because "God said so." Once you can get to the level of obeying God because He said so, you may eliminate a lot of your problems.

Now how do you get that way? You choose. I had to choose to do a lot of things that made absolutely no sense to me once I chose Christianity. I don't even remember most of them anymore because once I started doing them they were self-explanatory. The results were almost always a blessing, and even when they weren't, they were the result of obedience. When you choose correctly—now this is the foundational part—if you choose God, then God will choose you back and show you how and what you need to do. If you choose to believe the Bible, then read it with the intent to understand it and to do it. If the intent of your heart is correct and you choose God, then you allow God to do that which He would do this day. If you choose to obey the Bible and you choose to understand it, then God will give you the strength and the ability to do that choosing and to follow it through.

I could spend many pages telling you the terrible things I did before I became a believer. We've already gone over why you should listen to me, because I've walked there—I've been there—and the Lord has shown me how I survived for twenty-plus years undercover. Once I became a Christian, I said to Him, "Lord, what do I do now. . .what do I do about the bombs, the guns, the knives, the swords. . .what do I do about that?" And He said to me very clearly, "The disciplines of the flesh shall become the disciplines of the Spirit. Dare in my name as I show you." What I'm doing is what the Lord has shown me and that is how to translate my physical warfare into spiritual warfare. It wasn't by bouncing up and down in training and sports and living "up here" all the time. Choose that which you will do.

I had twenty-one years of Hebrew seminary and a couple of degrees in Christianity, but they mean nothing. What is important is I've been healed from many major diseases. They told me I'd never be out of a wheelchair again. They told me I'd be dead by the end of 1992. What has that got to do with this? I chose to obey the Word of God. The Word of God says believe, receive, be healed, and be made whole. Was it easy? Is it easy? I'm still being healed. Do I walk with a cane anymore? No, but did I? Several years ago I hobbled in and I hobbled out and I'm not hobbling anymore!

Focus on whether you desire in your heart of hearts to serve the Lord God this day. Whether you really believe—these are choosings. They're not choices, they're choosings. Decide if you want to stay where you are in the mediocre world of believers, unbelievers and make-believers. You can pick and choose where you are. You need to understand that there is a war between good and evil going on in the world today. The Lord in the heavens with His hosts has to fight that war, and you need to decide whether you are in the army of God, because if you're a believer, you're in it whether you like it of not. Decide whether you will have the full armor, whether you will wear that armor, and whether you are fully protected by your faith and belief. You're saved by grace through faith (Ephesians 2:8), and you don't have to do a thing except to receive the Messiah.

Do you want to be able to stand before the flame — so that it will wash over you and do no harm? Then you need to choose all these things and begin to understand that which we're talking about. Think about whether God is God, whether the Word of God is accurate as written. Think about whether the Messiah is really so. Think about whether the Holy Spirit has a connection with you and everything you do. Don't worry about tomorrow for there is evil sufficient unto this day. Don't worry but fulfill this day with the Lord God.

Remember that the Word of God is not just an instruction manual; it is God Himself! If you are seeking the Lord, all out and all over, don't look so far. Pick up the Bible and open it! The front cover says "The Holy Bible." He Himself is in there and He Himself is in the Word. The Word is God and He is with you. The Lord God is the truth. Remember as you choose God this day, "And ye shall know the truth, and the truth shall make you free." (John 8:32)

Choice is not a decision you make. Choice is something you get when you choose correctly. You must choose God, you must choose the Bible, you must choose the Holy Spirit, and you must choose your salvation. YOU must choose it, or you will not get the choice.

Chapter 4

COMMIT TO OBEY

*N*ow we will look at what you need to do and who you need to be, because in spiritual warfare you need to know who you are, what you are, and what you have to do. You need to look at your commitment to obey. What does it mean to obey? It's a covenant with God. The Bible is your instruction manual and it contains choice information. This is the best information you're going to find anywhere in the world to bring you to where you need to be, which is in power, in health, in happiness, and in a full day of goodness, this day!

Listen to me, as it is very simple. Most of you will know these things, and if you don't, you need to know them. However, most of you don't know them on a foundational level. I'm not telling you you're not intelligent, I'm telling you that you're probably too intelligent! Start bringing it down to a child-like level of understanding. I drive people in my congregation crazy, and I drive other people insane by bringing them into the understanding of the simplicity of God's Word. You know it's easy to get into high levels of understanding and all the great words and everything, but I say to you, "Find the most basic understanding."

When you commit to obey, you covenant with God. This is one of the most terrible and important things you have to understand. A covenant is not a promise; it is way more than a promise! A covenant is your heart commitment to God. You can look at unbelievers doing terrible things and they seem very successful to you.

You wonder why they're successful because they didn't covenant with God. Their punishment may come tomorrow, it may come at the end of their lives, or it may come whenever it comes, but their punishment will come.

YOU have covenanted with God. You've said "Yes, Lord!" If you've received the Lord as your Messiah and you've not done anything else, you have covenanted with God. Everything that comes out of your mouth and that is in your heart—God hears. That is a covenant. When you don't do what you say you break a covenant, not just a promise. Many people call it a covenant promise, but "covenant" means that God is in on it, and when you break it you break your promise to God. There are consequences. If you read your instruction manual you'll see what these consequences are. If you commit to obey, you covenant to obey Him, and make the decision. First you choose and what is your choosing? You will obey God.

Now this is a decision and not something you do. What did you get? You received God. Now isn't that the best? After you have decided — what then? You commit to obey and covenant with God to do that which He has commanded us this day. How do you do that? You learn the Word of God; you do the Word of God- NOW!!! Deuteronomy 27 says to obey the Lord your God to do that which He commands you this day. How is this different from the obedience of the world?

For example, I have a job at a TV station and I agreed to run a camera. The manager comes in and says to me, "I don't want you to run a camera, I want you to go back there and I want you to run the control board. If I know how, I agree. My obedience is conditional upon my agreement. I come back the third day, and I guess he wasn't thrilled with my job and he says, "You see that waiting room out there for people who are going to come be on the show? I want you to clean it everyday so they'll be happy and thrilled." Now I turn and look at the boss and I say, "You know what? No!" Now I have chosen not to obey because it is my right not to agree to do that. I can say "No." Now of course there are repercussions. He could tell me "OK, you don't have to," or "You're fired! Get outta here!" Let me say it again- my obedience is conditional upon my agreement.

Let me tell you a story about why the Hebrews received the Bible from the Lord God in the first place. This is a Hebrew tradition, which may or may not be historically correct. It's a great example either way. God came to the various tribes and He said to them (paraphrasing), "Here is the Bible!" He tried to give it to different groups of people, though not the Hebrews first. He came to all the other peoples and said to them (again, paraphrased), "You know what? Here's the Bible." They asked Him, "What's in it?" God said to each of them, "If you need to know you can't have it." Then God went to the Abraham and said, "Here's the Bible," and he said, "Thank you, we'll take it. We'll do it and then we'll know." The Hebrew people were created through Abraham for the purpose of serving God because Abraham committed to obey.

Many Jews who were not brought up in their faith are accepting the Lord God today. Through an overt decision, there are many Jews coming back to their Judaism. In fact, so many have come back to their faith that others have written special books teaching the Jews how to do all the traditions. Once a Jew says, "Yes, I accept Abraham, Isaac and Jacob, I accept the book of Moses, I accept the Bible" (what we call the Old Testament), then he no longer makes a decision to obey or not. When a Jew makes the commitment to accept the Lord God as their Lord and Savior, then he no longer makes decisions. The task from now on is committing to obey, coming into obedience and seeking the Lord, learning what He wants you to do and doing it. It's that simple.

Chapter 5

HEAR AND DO

*W*hen I became a brand-new believer, I knew nothing of Christianity but I knew that the Messiah was Jesus. I didn't know anything about Yeshua. I didn't know anything about Messianic Judaism. I just became a Christian, but I knew I was a Christian. I was an Old Testament Christian. I believed in the Bible, in every Word whether I understood it or not. I'd have Christians come up to me and say, "You know, I know I'm supposed to do this, but I'm not ready." I used to go crazy when I heard this!

I'd ask them a question. "Do you know that this is what the Word of God says?" They'd say, "Yes." Then I'd ask, "Do you understand it?" If they would say no, to the best of my ability I would teach them, and re-teach them if necessary. I had all the patience in the world to do that. If their answer was "Yes. . .Yes- I understand it, and I know God says it. . .but. . ." Well first of all I'm told by some real comedians that "but" is what you slide down to hell on. They say, "But I was told such and such." Well that drove me crazy. I would say, "How can you know that the Word of God is accurate as written? It's true, you say you believe it's true and you won't do it!" It drove me crazy and I wasn't very compassionate.

If you truly believe that God is God, that the Bible is accurate as written, that the Messiah is Jesus/Yeshua, that the Holy Spirit is here, and that God is in charge of your life - your breath, your provision, your health, and your happiness, then how would you dare disobey? I think I was a believer for about five days and was asked to speak from the pulpit. I said, "You don't really believe God is God. You believe there IS a God, but you don't believe that God is God, because if you believed, you would do it." No longer make decisions to do or not to do. Ask yourself a question. Should I do it, could I do it, would I do it?

I've never seen the word "maybe" in the Bible. Has anyone seen the word "maybe" in the Bible? Instead, I see words such as "commitment" or "obey" or "obedience." What is the difference between obedience and obey? You can get fancy and say one is the result of the act and one is the action, but that's not what we're talking about. Let's take a look at Deuteronomy 27:10, "Thou shalt therefore obey the voice of the Lord thy God, and do His commandments and His statutes, which I command thee this day," then the Word goes on to bless you, and comes and overtakes you, and all kinds of great and wonderful things will happen if you obey the Lord your God.

You need to remember what God has said to you. It's one of His many, many promises that the Messiah has come to fulfill: obey the Lord your God. Open your Bible up and have a paper and pencil handy as you never know when God's going to bring a little tidbit, because first He talks to you through the Bible. Then He talks to you from any media that you're willing to listen to, whether it is a billboard, a camera or even people talking to you. You need to be able to take notes and look it up.

The Lord said that you should fear the Lord your God, and keep all His statutes and commandments (Deuteronomy 5:26), which you are commanded to do. God doesn't ask you — He doesn't say please obey that which I give you this day. He commands us in every Word. How do I obey the Lord my God? I choose to do it. What are my actions? What does it mean, "I choose to do it?" I take actions based upon my decision to do that. I'm choosing, and what will I get if I choose to obey? God says that if I choose to obey, to keep all the statutes, that the days of my life and my children, and my children's children shall be made longer. They will be prolonged. (Exodus 6:1-2)

What does the phrase "to observe all" mean? It doesn't mean to look upon them. It means to do, to carry out all that He has commanded us to do, and then He'll give us what He's promised us in "a land flowing with milk and honey." God has promised you the best of the best. Sometimes I've had the best of the worst, as it seems I've found myself in terrible situations and terrible positions, and yet

I was guaranteed the best of even the worse! God will take care of us whether we're out in the street, whether we're in prison or whatever situation we find ourselves in. He'll take care of us because He said He would if we obey.

What do I have to do to obey? I have to know what God wants. How can we know what He wants? God will tell us through the Holy Spirit. Whether we walk around, or sit in a dark corner somewhere or whether we get into our prayer closets, we need to find a quiet place to pray. The Lord said, "In the beginning was the Word, and the Word was with God, and the Word is God." (John 1:1) Remember when you seek God, the Bible is where He is. "In the beginning was the Word. . ." this is where you seek the Lord first.

You may hear the Lord in many other places but the Bible is where you seek Him first, and if this is God, then this is the truth. You must choose to believe that! The way we learn to obey is by reading the manual, and to do the dos and not to do the don'ts. If you do all the dos by the time you get around to the don'ts you're not going to want to do them anyway. That's the Lord's truth!

It is empowering to look at the word for "obey" used in the Hebrew. Deuteronomy 6:1-3 (Tanach) says, "This is the command-ment, and the decrees, and the ordinances that HASHEM, your God, commanded to teach you, to perform in the Land to which you are crossing, to possess it, so that you will fear HASHEM, your God, to observe all His decrees and commandments that I com-mand you — you, your child, and your grandchild — all the days of your life, so that your days will be lengthened. You shall hearken, O Israel, and beware to perform, so that it will be good for you, and so that you will increase very much, as HASHEM, the God of your forefathers, spoke for you — a land flowing with milk and honey."[1]

Every Hebrew word has multiple meanings that are deter-mined by the context of the sentence. When I first became a believer I thought about rewriting Strong's Concordance. It would have taken years! Now there is a Bible program with multiple meanings for every word. There are nine different meanings of the word "obey" alone. The word "obey" used in the King James Version is "hearken" in the Stone Edition Tanach. In Hebrew this word is "lishmoa," meaning, "to hear and do." What's the difference? It assumes that the covenant has already been made. The believer is listening for instructions and will do them. Hear and do!

I want to remind you again- choose and receive the choice. Commit to obey. Make your covenant with the Lord God, and obey the Lord your God this day. Hear what He says in His Word and do it.

Chapter 6

OBEY, SUBMIT, BE HUMBLE

𝒩𝓮𝓼

The Messiah lived at the time when the priests in the temple did blood-sacrifice. Only through blood-sacrifice could you be healed; only through blood-sacrifice could you be made whole; and only through blood-sacrifice could you be forgiven. According to the Word of God, only through blood-sacrifice at the temple could any good thing happen to you. The temple was a living and active temple according to the laws in the Old Testament when the Messiah came. The entire teaching of the Messiah's people (our people, your people) was that you must go to the temple and you must sacrifice. He Himself went to the temple for all of the festivals. He didn't abandon His blessings. He didn't abandon His time.

The Word says in First Samuel 15:22, "To obey is better than sacrifice." In John 14:15 the Messiah says, "If you love me, keep my commandments." It's a Scripture no one wants to hear. He explained the commandment, "Love thy neighbor as thyself," in Matthew 22:39. You don't want to be loved like I love myself sometimes. The Messiah also explained, "This is my commandment, that ye love one another, as I have loved you." (John 15:12) This is the way you love someone, and this is the way you obey. You obey the Lord your God, by seeking to learn the Word as He has commanded you, and to do the Word that He's given you this day.

There are promises in His Word. He promises He will do for you if you do this. Understand again that your salvation is not based upon your works; it is based on obedience of one thing. You must receive the Giver, don't you ever forget that! You must believe and receive that the Messiah is Lord, and that He has the power to save you from sin and death. If you remember that, then you go on seeking the Word of God, and hear what He has to say. Remember that you hear God as you read the Bible. He wrote the book and every Word is His, and this instruction manual is from Him.

I would have liked to title this chapter "Learning how to spit in the devil's face!" What are our foundational points we need to have in order to conduct spiritual warfare? The only way we do that is in God's army. Whether we like it or not, if you are a believer in the Messiah, you are in God's army. If you're going to be shot at, if the devil is going to come and get you anyway, you might as well stand empowered—with strength, with joy, with happiness, and with direction!

There is a difference between obedience and obey. Obey is to covenant with God so that you will hear Him. Obedience is when you seek to do that which He has commanded you this day, and the intent of your heart is to do that which He commands you this day. Now what do we need to do to be obedient? It's a very simple word, and you're not going to like it. What you need to do is to submit. In Romans 6:16 the Lord says to us, "Know ye not, that to whom ye yield yourself servants to obey, His servants ye are to whom ye obey; whether of sin unto death, or of obedience unto righteousness?"

If we see what God is saying to us, that in our choosing (the very foundation that we're talking about), if you choose to obey satan whether you are a believer, a non-believer or even a make-believer, then you are willingly a servant of satan! We have to understand that if you do not serve God, then by default you serve satan! This is what the Lord says in the above Scripture verse in Romans, that the servant of sin- if you serve anything other than God—whatever it is—reaps the death of sin. If you serve the Lord—you choose to serve the Lord—then you reap the choice, the best of which is life everlasting.

There is a difference between obedient Hebrews and many of us today. Once a Hebrew has chosen to obey, which is a choosing, he no longer makes a daily decision to obey. Anyone who has made a decision to follow Christ should pay attention. If you said that prayer, "I became a believer; I now seek the Lord—I want to hear what He has to say and do." Let me give you a Scripture reference. The Lord will bless thee, as Deuteronomy 15:5 says, "Only if thou carefully hearken unto the voice of the Lord thy God, to observe to do all these commandments which I command thee this day." The Scripture does not say to obey and to do; it says to hear (hearken) and to do. I and you (I hope) have already made the decision to obey God and obey Him till the end.

Now, I have to learn. I have to get into the Word of God to learn what there is to do. I obey the Scripture that says that I come before thee and open my mouth and let the Lord speak (paraphrasing Matthew 10:20). What you've been reading so far, you can find in the Word of God and if you can't, then don't do it! In other words, I do it because God is and I do it because He said so. I do it because I know that's what I'm supposed to do, and in my recognition that I can't do it any other way.

How do I submit to God? I have to go back to the first part and agree that He is God. In order to understand that He is God, I need to know that He IS the Lord. Then if He IS the Lord God, I have to get into the second part, which is about humbling myself in the sight of the Lord. James 4:10 tells us: "Humble yourselves in the sight of the Lord, and He shall lift you up." People may say to you, "Well you're a mind-numbed robot and this is a crutch." Well you know something? If this is a crutch, I want two of them. If I could figure out how to use three of them I would!

You need to be humble before God. Humble does not mean weak. You can be a powerful and mighty man or woman of God, but understand who is in charge. In the Word of God, He has promised us long life, that your life may be pro-longed, and not just you and me, but our children and our children's children (Deuteronomy 6:2). When He told this to our forefathers He spoke of their forefathers, and this promise is committed all the way through, even up until this day. Anybody who tells you that this is for the past is a liar or deceived. I won't say he's of the devil; he's just being used and misused.

Now about the word humble. One day I was teaching in the state of Washington. I was a brand-new believer then, and I had just gone into a service and sat down. This man got in the pulpit, pointed his finger at me and said; "Now that's a humble man before God!" I turned around to see the person he was talking about, because I was even louder then than I am now. I was even bigger in size than I am now. I just thought I was a big ol' loudmouth! I didn't understand. . .I mean I just didn't shut up for God!

I wanted to find out what this man meant because he wouldn't tell me what it meant to be "humble unto the Lord." I went to the dictionary. Now what the dictionary says is humble is the "state of being meek," so I looked up meek. Meek is the "state of being humble." Now there are all kinds of other meanings, but it didn't mean anything to me at the time. I already understood from the Word of God that humble does not mean weak. I have never been able to walk around "meekly." I'll lower my head before the Lord. There's a word in Hebrew called "hashkiveinu," where you prostrate yourself on the floor before the Lord. I won't do it before man, but I will surely do it before the Lord anytime—just like that!

What the heck is humble? I told you before; I choose to do what the Bible says, because when I became a Christian I wouldn't even take communion for the first five months because I didn't know what it meant. It says in the Scriptures not to take of the bread and drink of the cup "unworthily." (First Corinthians 11:27) The Word also says if you bring a gift to the altar and remember that ". . .thy brother hath ought against thee; leave there thy gift before the altar, and go thy way; first be reconciled to thy brother. . ." and then offer your gift! (Matthew 5:23-24) You know you have got to lay it before the altar, and I'm talking forgiveness here. I didn't know what it meant to "lay it before the altar." It took me five months to figure out what it meant; when I finally understood, I took communion.

I needed to know what this man who said I was "humble" meant. What I finally found out is that to humble yourself before God is to submit and to acknowledge He is God. He is the Supreme Being. Now we have acknowledged that He is God and we've acknowledged that He is the Supreme Being. What do I do in that acknowledgment? This man saw something, but I had no clue. It's because I was brought up since childhood in the Word of God. I had an understanding of God. No matter how prideful I might have been in my doings, I understood something that is so basic. If you understand this, your life gets real easy. Humble is the full and complete understanding that I can do nothing without God, and that I am nothing without God.

I'm not talking about putting my head down and walking around and saying, "Woe is me, I ain't nothin', I ain't nobody." Once we understand that all the goodness we have—every proper and good and positive thing that we do—that God has granted us the ability and power to do that! Anything that I can do, even the fact that I can walk, is a miracle! Now I didn't heal myself; I didn't deliver myself! I shouldn't be able to walk- I have no toes on one foot, but I can stand up on that foot with no real problems. God has granted me the ability and power to do that. God gives me my breath, as I've had four lung diseases, yet I can blow a shofar. I couldn't walk up a flight of stairs without having to rest for thirty minutes. They told me in 1992 that I would be dead within a year. God has done everything and I have agreed; I have been willing!

I submit to God, I submit to the Word, and I come to the humble understanding that all that I have is from God. All that I will be is for God — all the strength I have, every breath I take and everything I do. This is not preaching, this is the truth and this is the fact. This is the foundation that you must acquire and you must realize that.

Chapter 7

COME AS A CHILD

*W*e talk about coming as a child. First Corinthians 13:11 says, "When I was a child, I spake as a child, I understood as a child, I thought as a child; but when I became a man, I put away childish things." Everyone thinks you've got to hurry up and grow up, but what you need to do as a believer is become a child of God.

Let me give you an example. Let's say you have a child (a year or two old) and they're now walking and talking. You're in a house and he's standing at the top of a flight of stairs and you say, "Son— hey you—Jump! He looks at you and he laughs, and he hesitates, and then he flings himself off the top of the stairs. You go, "Ohhh!" and you catch him. Now if you catch him, and he doesn't hurt himself, he will do it from that moment on. Why? Because your child trusts you and has faith—absolute faith!

This is why it's so important that when we have children not to hurt them and to teach them that all the good and everything they get from us comes from God. The first time the child jumped is because he loves you and trusts you. He had this basic hesitation but then it's "I'm gonna do it!" Bam! From then on the jumping is that the child is proving himself to you, but the first jump has to be because you're his father and he first trusted you.

The same goes for God. Sometimes we need to take that leap. God is our Father; we need to learn to trust. Faith is belief and trust that God will do what He says He will do. When you have a child you must convey the warmth and goodness that mother and daddy provide, and you must make it clear to the child that it is from God. As they grow up and as we grow up, how do you come to God as a child? How can you do all this choosing, and obedience, and obeying, and submitting and being humble—how can you do all these things without question?

It's with the understanding that if God says, "Stand in front of the flame," do it! You may recall the fiery furnace in the book of Daniel. If not, this is the time to read it. This is what we're teaching now because I'm expecting a real physical flame, not just a spiritual flame. One day you may have to trust God to stand before the flame, and if you do not stand, you'll burn.

I once took a test in the Israeli Secret Service. You stood against a wall and three healthy guys took new, hard tennis balls and started throwing them at you. You were supposed to defend yourself, but there was no way to win this one. Of course when you first take the test, you don't know that. They're throwing and you're getting pounded. If you're really good they get more guys and more tennis balls, and you eventually end up on the floor curled up to protect yourself, and the test is over. What you don't know is that if you turn your back while you're going down, they throw you out. They don't expect you to succeed all the time, but what they expect you to do is to go down facing the enemy.

God wants something even easier. He doesn't even expect you to go down. What He expects you to do is to stand without question—as a child, as a child throws himself off the balcony and into your arms. This is what God wants from you, absolute trust as a child. A child trusts without conditions. The only way the rest of this foundational, spiritual warfare preparation works is if you do it because He's God. You believe because He said so, and you obey the Word because it's His Word.

You can have intelligent and in-depth understandings, and you should continue learning, but you know the old saying "Why should I do what my mom says?" It's "because." I used to get crazy when she would tell me "because." As a little child I learned not to act up in public because she'd give me a little smack! Now God doesn't smack you, He just doesn't save you. You have salvation (if you've accepted the Messiah), but if you're in disobedience, He doesn't save you from the repercussions of your disobedience of the day.

If I truly understand as a child that God is God, then there's no other way that I could do this. There's no other way I could do this under my own power. This is where simple basic sentences come from. The devil tries to complicate them, and man tries to complicate them. You know why man tries to complicate them? Because if they're complicated, then they don't have to do it! They have absolute excuses. You understand? Absolute excuses for not doing what they need to do!

You need to learn, to study and do. Yes, you must be a meat-eater (Hebrews 5:14) and bring the Word into your heart, but you must obey as a child- without question, without hesitation, without a why. No whys- you do it because God said so. You must come in the absolute and full forgiveness of the Lord your God. He is so merciful!

Chapter 8

FORGIVE

*L*et's talk about forgiveness. You say, "When I became a believer they told me I need to forgive everyone, so I ran around and I forgave them." There's only one person that most of us seem to forget (at the beginning especially), and that's to forgive YOU. Forgiving one's self is difficult. If you do not forgive yourself as the Word says you should, then — first of all — you're in disobedience to God. You have no right not to forgive yourself anymore than I would have the right not to forgive someone if they did anything wrong.

I must forgive because God said so and I must forgive myself. I'm calling God a liar if I do not forgive myself because God says that in my salvation I am cleansed, I am made new, and I rise up a new creature! "Therefore if any man be in Christ, he is a new creature: old things are passed away; behold, all things are become new." (Second Corinthians 5:17) I don't want to call God a liar. We must continue to do the acts we did when we first became believers. What do we do? We ask forgiveness, receive forgiveness and then we repent.

There are many people who think that repentance is forgiveness. No, no, no! We repent second, first we ask forgiveness. However it's not enough to ask forgiveness, you have to receive forgiveness and of course you have to forgive. I know people who have forgiven everyone in the whole world — including dogs that bark at them — and never get around to forgiving themselves. You have to receive forgiveness for yourself. You have to believe you are

39

forgiven. There is nothing that I have done in my life that God isn't big enough to forgive. He's promised me that in His Word.

Now we come to repentance. Everyone knows that repentance means to turn from the action or activity that caused us to sin. But, where do you turn to? What it means to repent is you're basically saying, "Ma, I stole a cookie- forgive me." She says, "Okay, I forgive you." "Okay Ma, I receive the forgiveness. I will not steal the cookie anymore." But what do I do now? What do I do that is good? I am turning from sin. What am I turning to?

I am turning to the Word of God. The most important part after recognizing that God IS and that I will forgive myself is to read the Word of God. Look in the Word of God and fit everything in your life into the Bible.

Chapter 9

PRACTICE

You must practice giving God the credit and doing what the Word tells you to do. For instance, when I was training anti-terrorist units in Israel, I was the second best shot in Israel. I didn't just do it by sitting around. I practiced hours and hours, and days and days. I practiced all the time. When I got out of the military, I had to practice not worrying that people would be jumping out of holes somewhere. I had to practice allowing you to walk up to me in the dark and poke me in the back, without knocking you down.

If you're a typist you practice on your typewriter. If you're a marksman you practice shooting. If you're an assassin you practice many skills. If you're a cameraman you learn to use your camera. You know what to do to test it out, and then you do it. You walk it out. Some people say, "I'm a believer, I received the Holy Spirit!" and then they don't do anything about it. They don't practice.

After becoming a believer, I realized I shouldn't curse anymore. I used to be able to curse in almost fifteen languages! I had to practice not to curse. I had to practice and I had to realize, "How do I become a believer? What is required?" I had to retrain my reflexive conditioning. In martial arts they say, "If you have to think about it, it's too late." It's the same thing with spiritual warfare.

Let's say you're driving in a car and you see another car coming and you realize you are both on solid ice. The other guy has hit the brakes, and you've got nowhere to go because you are on the same ice. There are piles of snow and you're looking over. . .what is the first thing to come into your mind? "Oh horse manure!" Well, that's not going to get you very far! Who is the only one who is going to save you? Cry out to Him.

This happened to me years ago, in the middle of winter. A car headed straight toward me and I prayed "JESUS!" and covered my eyes and there was no big smash! When I opened my eyes the car was stopped within inches. I couldn't even get out from the driver's side, we were that close! We weren't even going to risk moving the cars because we were still on solid ice. The other driver couldn't figure out why he didn't smash into the side of my car! What was my reaction? Was it the stuff that the horse puts on the floor or did I cry out to my Messiah? Why did I cry out to Him? Because I had practiced it! I didn't sit there doing nothing; you have to work at conditioning.

We have great sayings like, "Learn to walk the walk and talk the talk," but how do you do these things? How do you bind the enemy? How do you loose the angels in the heavenlies to come help you? How do you do these things? First you need to be submitted foundationally to God. You need to understand that God can do it, otherwise God won't. The Lord says very clearly that He is giving you the ability to choose. He doesn't force you to do anything. The key—and what I'm trying to help you learn as I have learned—is that the power and might on this earth is yours today!

As you choose the Lord and commit to obey Him, you move into the obedience of what the Lord would have you do, and then submit unto Him in that doing. Humble yourself to the point where you truly understand, and you truly believe that the Messiah is Lord. He—and only He—is the One who is doing the work within you. If you can do this and follow through, you will begin to be a Mighty Warrior in the Lord! You don't have to buy a sword and you don't have to get a gun. He is our Protector with the flaming sword—the flaming Sword of the Spirit! That's the Sword of our Lord, the Word of God! The Word of God must be active in you and in me!

Chapter 10

WARRIORS IN TRAINING

𝕭𝕰

O ne of the things that the Lord has shown me is that there is a season for everything. (Ecclesiastes 3:1) We're coming into the season of the end of the beginning. The Lord has been preparing us to come into what people call the "end times," or even the "new millennium." Call it whatever you want, but what is going on in the world today is "spiritual warfare." It's a war between good and evil. The time and place on earth today is that the spirit is manifesting itself in the flesh, but the real war is in the spirit. In Ephesians, Scripture tells us where this war is taking place. "For we wrestle not against flesh and blood, but against principalities, against powers, against the rulers of the darkness of this world, against spiritual wickedness in high places." (Ephesians: 6:12)

If you are a believer today, then you're part of God's army. Whether you like it or not, you're in the war. Decide whether or not you want to be a soldier who doesn't take training seriously. You will find yourself in the depths of combat, ill equipped and terrified because you know not what to do. Remember you have all the abilities and potential possibilities to be great and to survive willingly, happily and joyfully!

I've been doing Christian television and radio shows for a long time and some people tell me I need to be a bit more proper. You don't have to be proper! "The joy of the Lord is your strength!" (Nehemiah 8:10) The Word says "Rejoice. . .and again I say, Rejoice!" (Philippians 4:4). This is NOT a request! None of the commandments of God are requests! God commands you — He says to "Rejoice!" He doesn't say "Rejoice if you have had a good day."

Joy is not necessarily happiness, but the knowledge and understanding that God is God, that the Messiah is Lord, and that the Word is our REAL instruction manual. If you read the back of the book you'll find that once we're through these tribulations, WE WIN! We wait for the Millennial Kingdom, we wait for the Messiah to come, and we wait for the joy and happiness, yet we live in a time today when we can have Kingdom on earth! "Thy Kingdom come. Thy will be done, in earth as it is, in heaven." (Matthew 6:10)

God has promised us joy, happiness, provision, fulfillment, and healing. We can have blessedness together as one in the body, one in the Spirit, with one mind and having one goal. The goal is to bring Salvation to all those who do not know Him, and to bring fullness to those who do know Him.

Now maybe you've been trained in spiritual warfare to yell and cast out devils and demons. The results of your training will cause it to happen. You know, one of the things I wanted to do it since I was a brand-new believer is that people would be healed when our shadows touched them. Read Acts 5:15. Did not Peter do this? That as we walk into the room, evil would flee! That the devil would go away by our very presence! Now you say "Rabbi, is that not presumptuous?" I'm here because the Lord took me through physical and spiritual experiences that have brought me to an understanding that it is simple! The foundations of the Holy Spirit, the foundations of Spiritual warfare are simple if you understand what you need to do — if you understand who you are — if you understand that God is in you!

We need to begin to focus on how to win. First you have to be trained. Soldiers have to be trained before they can be effective. YOU must be trained as a spiritual warrior! You don't have to leave your home; you can be a mother, a father, a grandfather; you can be in a wheelchair. You can be a warrior of the Lord! I said that before I was a believer, I was a Warrior of David, and I was! I hunted the enemies of Israel. Today I'm still a Warrior of David, but I'm also a Warrior through the Messiah and God in heaven. I'm a Warrior of David through God and the power of the whole Bible, which is my instruction manual.

How do I move into the action phase? I look to the Word — the Bible. Yes — the Holy Spirit speaks, and He still speaks today, and yes I've heard God audibly. You can ask God to speak to you audibly, but the foundational understanding and the hearing of God are in the Word. "But what if it's the wrong version?" you ask. "What if they interpreted it incorrectly? I heard they put the commas and the periods in the wrong place." Just choose God. Once you've committed to obey, in the choosing you have to believe that He is big enough, He is strong enough and He is the Word! If He IS the Word, then if you seek Him by the Holy Spirit, He will bring you into understanding in the Word.

Some say the Holy Spirit is of the devil, so I ask them, "If the Holy Spirit is of the devil why didn't the devil give it to me when I was serving him?" God may speak to you in the spirit through the Holy Spirit, but everything that Holy Spirit says to you needs to be verified in the Word. If you can't find something in the Word that the Spirit said to you, I would question how holy that spirit is. This is not a joke. The devil can imitate even the light, but what he cannot do is stand against the name of the Lord. When the Holy Spirit does speak to you, or God speaks to you directly, He will never contradict His Word. He will never add to His Word, or take away from His Word. What is in the Word is THE Word—immovable, irrevocable, better than the mountains and the seas and the stone.

I used to hate Christians. When I was thirty-nine years old, I found out that God loved me so much that He spread His arms out, and in His death and resurrection spoke to me audibly so that I could sit here and tell you that God is God and that Jesus is Lord! We have learned these things so you can have the foundation to begin as a true soldier and warrior—man, woman, and child. You are now a warrior of God so that you can go forth and fulfill your commitment to the Lord.

Chapter 11

STAND BEFORE THE LORD

*W*e've been talking about how to join God's army. We need now to stand before the Lord, or we will wind up kneeling before the enemy! You say, "Rabbi, isn't that a bit drastic? Is this the Holy Roller fire and brimstone stuff that if you don't do this or that you're going to end up in hell?" We're not talking about hell; we're talking about hell on earth!

One of the words that God has been giving us for this time is that the end of the beginning is at hand. In church there are believers, and out in the world there are unbelievers, and somewhere in the middle—most of the time in church—are the make-believers. The make-believers are the ones who are in the most danger, because they've covenanted. One who stands in church and says, "I love You Lord," and then says, "Yes I will," and then doesn't is in deep trouble. That's because there are covenant conditions. You're saved by grace through faith, and you can't be more saved or less saved. You can have His grace and His power and His might!

We're not talking about taking up a sword and we're not talking about running around the street screaming and yelling. What we're talking about is the mighty war in the heavens! Whether you like it or not, there is a war on. There are many believers who think, "Oh, I did a terrible thing." The devil is yelling in your ear that God won't take you back. Maybe you think you are "kind of" saved, but there's something in a little corner in the back of your mind that's stopping you from knowing for sure. What does this have to do with spiritual warfare?

In a time of war, if there are cracks in your armor, the devil sneaks in. I promise you, if you go to the battlefield today, and you take a look at an armored Humvee or a tank, you'll see the armor is extended further out, and it's getting thicker and better. A lot of soldiers would be dead now if the armor hadn't been strengthened. It is the exact same thing in spiritual warfare! You are in danger if you have cracks in your understanding of God—if you have crevices in your faith—but you say, "Oh, I'm a believer and I have faith in God, I know who God is!" You have to make sure you know that you know that God is God, that Yeshua is Jesus! God is the Father, He is the Son, and He is the Holy Spirit—the Word is real. This is your armor. Otherwise you're wasting your energy. We are in a time and place in the world that evil is taking its last stand against good, but goodness is being poured out across the earth.

Remember—the war is not against flesh and blood, but against spirits and principalities of darkness in high places. (Ephesians 6:12) To paraphrase First Peter 5:8, the devil wanders about as a roaring lion to see whom he may devour. The word "may" is important. If you are a believer, you must give him permission. Do not give him permission! God sanctions the devil's job, whether you like it or not. God gave the devil dominion over this earth and all therein. (Revelation 12:7-9) Then God turned to us and said, "Now is come salvation, and strength, and the kingdom of our God, and the power of His Christ: for the accuser of our brethren is cast down, which accused them before our God day and night." (Revelation 12:10)

The Messiah reminds us that we will do even greater works than He did! (John 14:12) Going back to Genesis, "Then God blessed them, and God said to them, 'Be fruitful and multiply; fill the earth and subdue it, have dominion. . .'"(Genesis 1:28) "Subdue" means to take by force or to bend to the will. We want "our will" to be done. This is what satan is doing today—he's taking us away from God's will and he's trying to create our own understanding of our will. Subdue is to bring it to the will of God by His Word and through His Holy Spirit.

Today this is what this war is about. It has never changed. I don't care who persecuted the Jews or the Christians; the persecutors were driven by evil. Their desire is not as much to destroy the people, as to destroy the people's faith in God. Since the times of the

Romans and throughout history, how many times have you heard "If you don't want to be thrown to the lions all you have to do is renounce Christ?" In Spain during the Inquisition, Queen Isabella and her husband decided to make their country a Christian nation. If a Jew didn't convert, they cut off his head or even burned him at the stake. In every instance it's not the ultimate war against the person, it's against his belief in the one true living God and through our Messiah to that God. That's what it's all about today because the devil wants us to give up our faith, to give up our belief. Most important—and where he is succeeding—he wants to stop our actions.

Abraham (when he was still Abram) was the son of an idol-maker. If you weren't growing good crops, you prayed to the moon god and you prayed to the god of the earth. If that didn't work and you still weren't having good crops you went to the idol-maker and picked up a piece of wood. He then chipped and chopped the wood up and prayed some words over it, and then you took it and you prayed over it. If it worked, it was a great god. If it wasn't you threw it away and went and got another. Everyone believed in something. Everyone believed in something other than them-selves—in a higher authority.

Every time the devil has come in a great movement across the earth to destroy God's people, God has brought an even greater movement to stop it. But there has been a great price. Am I going to tell you this is the end times? No, it's not my business. God said He'll come as a thief in the night (2 Peter 3:10) and He says to be ready. Now bear with me — I can tell you exactly when Jesus is coming! You know how exciting that is? I can tell you EXACTLY when He's coming! Every time I say that, people start inching away from me and thinking, "Uh-oh, there's another nut-case! He doesn't know what he's doing; he thinks he knows. . ." But I do know! You know when He's coming? Today! The Messiah is coming today because what was yesterday when it was here? Today. What will tomorrow be? Today. When the Messiah does come, whether it be in a single day, or whenever it is down the road—that day will be Today.

Do you understand that the Messiah is and has and will come again soon? Do you understand that the Word is accurate as written and is your instruction manual? Do you know that the devil is trying to do you in? Do you understand that humanism is of the devil and is founded in the desire to drive you away from the Word of God? Do you understand that this IS strictly a war between good and evil, with winner take all? If not, then you're in deep trouble because sometime soon a wall of flame is going to come crashing across the earth. We're not talking metaphorically and we're not talking spiritually. We're talking for real! God asks the question, "Will you stand before the Lord, or kneel before the enemy?"

Everyone has a god of some sort. This is a trick of the devil by the way. In the late 1800's, humanists began to teach "I." They began to teach "Me." Humanism is still being taught today and will continue (unfortunately) over the next century, even the next millennium. How many times have you heard, "Well if the Holy Spirit is in me, and the Holy Spirit is God, and therefore God is in me, then I am God?" You hear this from some so-called Christians. You hear it out of the different dogmas of religions and cults that lead you into, "I AM GOD." Our educational system and has become controlled by humanists, and they teach that choice is okay. Whatever your choice is - whether you choose this or you choose that—it's your choice. As we learned earlier, this is a lie of the devil. Anything not of God is NOT choice!

I'm part of the 60's generation and I survived. Then I became a believer, which was far better. People who grew up in my generation have been to college and have been placed in positions of authority. They are now lawyers, doctors, judges and politicians with the sole purpose of getting God out of our country, and out of the world. That's what the war has been all through history; it's the war between good and evil, and it's going on today.

Chapter 12

THE ARMIES OF GOD

I believe that we're all Judeo-Christians, which means that Abraham was the Father of the nations (including us), and Yeshua was sent to us to save all of us. The Bible says in Isaiah 53:3 that the Messiah would be "despised and rejected." If all the Hebrews had believed that He was the Messiah, the prophecy would not have been fulfilled. Now we are beginning to come together, Judeo-Christians, Genesis to Revelation. I think we can agree that we are the descendants of the seed of Abraham and that we were freed from Egypt. Here is my question: Did God free the slaves from Egypt? Everyone will shout, "Yes!" The answer is "No!" Were the Hebrew slaves in Egypt? Yes! Did He free them as slaves? No!

This is the foundation of the continuation of the Armies of God. Rabbi, are you reading this correctly in the Word of God? It's the Bible, and it says, ". . . for in this selfsame day have I brought your armies out of the land of Egypt. . ." Open your Bible to Exodus 12:17. This is part of a teaching on Passover, but listen closely to what the Lord says in this passage of Exodus. "And ye shall observe the feast of unleavened bread; for in this selfsame day have I brought your armies out of the land of Egypt: therefore shall ye observe this day in your generations by an ordinance for ever." Wait—it gets better! If you look in other versions it says "hosts," "legions" or "divisions."

Let's go back to the original Hebrew. I like going there because it makes life a lot of fun! In the English translation of the Stone Edition of the Tanach, it says (from Hebrew), "You shall safeguard the matzos, for on this very day I will have taken your legions (tzva'ot) out of the land of Egypt. . ." Listen to what the Hebrew says which is really exciting. That one word in Hebrew actually means not just armies, but your armies. In Hebrew today, "Tzva HaHagana LeYisra'el" is the Israel Defense Forces- the Army of Israel!

God did not free people as slaves. The Hebrews had been slaves, but He freed them as the army! He freed us as the army! We are a continuation of the armies of God. Now are we supposed to go and conquer the land? Yes we are, but not physically. It began to happen with our Messiah, and then we were to continue to go across the land. We should have enough of an influence to bring people to the one true living God. Being a soldier in God's army is not a new thing. God created our people, Judeo-Christians, for the purpose of being His army.

You have to understand what disobedience has done to those of us in God's army. Ishmael was never supposed to be anything but another Semitic nation under Abraham and under the one true living God and the Messiah. Read the entire story in Genesis Chapter 16. If Hagar had taught her son properly and he had been obedient, he would have been the head and the prince of twelve tribes. He was denied the promise that was given to Isaac but he wasn't denied God's promise. Ishmael should have been an integral part of God's kingdom through his obedience, but eventually Islam showed up and they were totally outside of that obedience. If the people of the Arab nations had been obedient in 1947-48, followed the United Nations instructions and not invaded Israel, Palestine would be the same age as Israel. Yet there is disobedience, which is submission to evil and therefore submission to the enemy. The enemy is anything that is not God.

This is where we are today. God created the people of Judeo-Christianity for the purpose of being His army to take dominion over this earth and to bring His Word. The command of the Messiah was to go forth into the land and make ye disciples. (Matthew 28:19) We are to be disciples of God through the Messiah. The Messiah is waiting for those who need to come into His arms, so that they may stand with Him. You are a member of the army of God and now you've been taught to take dominion over this society and this world in His name so that we can have love, goodness, justice and righteousness in His Word, in His way and by His power and by His Love.

Chapter 13

RELEASE OF THE WARRIORS

O ur Messiah is Jewish and never converted to anything. He is our Judeo-Christian Savior. Yeshua was and is here for all of us. First of all, you must believe that He was born! That it was a virgin birth that was miraculous and that it was and is for believers only. The Jews weren't some tribe wandering around like the Hittites and the Amalekites and all the other "ites" out there in the desert. They were a people created through father Abraham. They were created for the purpose of one thing only, and that's to be the vessel of light for the world, a lamp unto thy feet and a light to the world.

Because of man's disobedience, the Messiah had to come to save us. God knew we would be such a stiff-necked people! God knew that He would have to send the Messiah so He wouldn't destroy the earth. What did the Messiah do? Did He just pop down here and do a couple of miracles? Did He look around and say, "OK, be like me and hit the road." No. The Messiah came to be an ensample. What is an "ensample" you ask? Well, God the Messiah Yeshua came in the flesh to show us how to act and conduct ourselves. Paul tells us in Philippians 3:17, "Brethren, be followers together of me, and mark them which walk so as ye have us for an ensample." Christ was our "ensample."

Why am I saying ensample instead of example? Why don't I just say example? Because—see my glasses? If I asked for an example of glasses anyone of you could give me your glasses—if you wear them. If I asked you for an ensample of these glasses, you have to give me an exact duplicate, down to the very smudge! The Messiah came to be an ensample and He showed us from birth on everything we need to know. You say, "Well we only know about His three years of ministry." That's because you're probably a Christian who's been taught that the Jews have nothing to do with it and there is no history. Hogwash! Baloney! Pastrami and Salami!

Everything has been written down! One of the twelve tribes of Israel — the Levites — was called to be scribes. God did not only call the Levitical tribe to be priests, but they were the scribes, and they wrote everything down. If you wrote everything the Messiah did, you would have hundreds or thousands of books. Yeshua's followers wrote enough that you would know the ensample, which is the purpose of the Messiah. You have to understand that He — the Messiah — empowered us! We have to be careful that we don't pray, "God, Oh God. . .please destroy this. . . oh stop that, oh fix this, this. . . that." Yes, we pray to God's will for God's will to be done. He empowers us in prayer to take dominion over everything. The hosts of heaven — the armies of God — can't move unless we pray.

Now I love swords, but don't think that you've got to pick up a sword and go hacking and flailing about, although if it wasn't for the mercy of our Messiah Yeshua some people would need a sword! The Koran commands its followers to cut off the heads of the infidels. You can actually go on the Arab sites on the Internet, where there are specific instructions on beheading according to the instruction of the Koran. Why am I telling you this? Am I yelling at Muslims? No. This isn't a war with people's names on it. We're fighting against evil. I don't hate them. I used to be an unsaved, orthodox Zionist national soldier. I was in the military; I was an assassin. I'm telling you today I still am an assassin but the difference is I'm assassinating evil — not people. I speak the truth. The only truth I know is the Bible.

If someone asks me what is right, Moshe no longer has his own opinion. Rabbi Moshe has a fact- and that fact is the Word of God. If it's in the Bible, then that's how I'm supposed to act. If my Messiah did it, I'm supposed to act that way also, and if He didn't, then I'm not. "Well, what if He didn't show us how?" You can find the solution to every problem that you have in the Bible. Now it might not be the solution you want or the answer you want to hear, but there is righteousness, power, goodness, happiness, health, wealth and provision in the Word of God! It's all there right from the beginning to the end.

Let's take a look at something in the Bible that you will find very interesting. Women, you are not just the "virtuous woman" of Proverbs 31:10! It's been mistranslated. The virtuous woman came from the King James translation. King James chose 400 rabbis and priests to translate the Bible from the original languages. The translation of "virtuous woman" came about because there was no way they were going to translate the real meaning. They weren't going to allow their women to know that they were what the Bible says they are.

The Stone Edition Tanach translation also weakens the meaning although not to the same extent. It says, "An accomplished woman who can find? Far beyond pearls is her value." I'll give you the Hebrew and then you can get excited! It says in Hebrew "eshet chayil." "Eshet" means wife and "chayil" means soldier- a warrior. You see how empowering that is? Virtuous woman properly translated means "warrior wife!"

What that means is your destiny is not just sitting around being passive and looking pretty. I actually have never understood how anybody could think how it was "virtuous woman." What does virtue have to do with carrying a side of beef from the gate up to the house, and taking care of the home, and being the foundation of the husband and the teachers of the children? Because you are to be the active support of your husband and to do God's will. You are very, very important! You are no less a warrior!

Every time I mention this, women take notice. Why? That doesn't mean you become the head of the household. It's like my bride. I would not be sitting here if it weren't for her. It's about her caring, her love. One of the main reasons we get along is it is not terribly important who's right and wrong. Being right or wrong is a big thing in many marriages for some reason, but what we should be thinking about is "Are we pleasing to God?"

In Old Testament times (and should be in our time), a newly married man could not leave his wife for a year even to go to war. (Deuteronomy 24:5) He could defend his home at the home. Heaven forbid that the war would even reach that far. Why isn't he permitted to leave his home for one entire year? First, the foundation of the family must be built. If you look at history you will see from the beginning that God created the family. Then he transferred power from the head of the family to the oldest son.

God sent His Son—the Messiah (our heavenly Father on earth)—to give us the power to take dominion over what we have and what we are. We take dominion over the evil on this earth and cast it into that dark, dark place where it belongs — because evil can only walk where we allow it! Do you understand that? Evil can only exist where good doesn't.

What's my job as a spiritual warrior today? We have been told to go into the world to make disciples (Matthew 28:19). Disciples of whom? Christ! Well, what are you supposed to do about it? What are you supposed to teach them to do? Go make more disciples! Believers know about Christ, and yet the devil is eating everybody's lunch! Look around you. Why?

The Messiah did not just bring salvation, He brought salvation and power and kingdom and might! He brought the ability and wisdom to take dominion over the earth and all therein—and subdue it unto His name! Evil is rampant, but the windows of heaven are open and the blessings are pouring down upon the earth! However, the majority of believers, however well intentioned, are teaching recognition of evil and nothing else. The power of God that is not being used is just like electricity that does nothing. A believer who is saved and does nothing is like electricity in a battery. It's like a 100 mega-watt station that can light up the city of New York but nothing is plugged into it. What a waste!

Your walk with the Lord is yours. You need to know the Messiah in your own understanding—in your own way. What you need to know is written in the Bible. People have said to me over the years, "The Holy Spirit told me that this is what it really means." Let me tell you something, it may have been a spirit, but it wasn't the Holy Spirit. God's Word is unchangeable and unchanging. Some may say, "Yeah, well man wrote it, and it contains mistakes." First of all man wrote it under God's anointed direct power; God is big enough that if man put a comma in the wrong place or is teaching incorrect dogma, mankind is not going to be completely misled. God is a big enough God to redirect us!

When I open up a Hebrew book I hear, "You opened it up backwards!" No I didn't. I opened it up the Hebrew way, which reads from back to front and from right to left. The English way is from left to right. We have the English way or the Hebrew way. Not right and wrong. Each person and each thing has its way. Everything in God's world has its place. Christianity and Judaism should be joined together as one in prayer. Today the only answer is the proper understanding of the position of how to pray and how to affect your life and the lives of those around you.

The United States Army has an advertising slogan. The slogan is "The Army of One." We have more than two million men and women under arms. When the publicists came up with "The Army of One," I don't think they understood how right on they hit it! Whether it's a hundred or its a million people, they are individuals working simultaneously for a just cause. This is what you need to become—"One" of millions and millions! One of like mind, like faith, like understanding and like power so that we can join together in that just cause. From the Word of God comes this truth, and from this truth comes power, and this power originates directly from God. Amen!

Chapter 14

EMPOWERED

I want to bring up an interesting point. It's something you may use the next time a Jewish person tells you that Yeshua is not our Messiah. They'll tell you "That's not our Messiah, our Messiah's still coming." Just tell them to ask Him when He gets here if it's the first time or the second time.

Now let's back up here. What's more important is that He was born into a Jewish family — miraculously, supernaturally! It had to be supernatural! We have the Messiah who was brought up in a Jewish household. He was apprenticed to His father, a carpenter. He lived life as a Jew. At the age of like twelve and a half — the best we can figure, because otherwise he wouldn't have been allowed — He went to the temple to celebrate the festival. With the festival over, Mary and Joseph pack up and leave. They're halfway back to where they were going and say, "Where's Yeshua?" They turn around.

I used to live in Jerusalem and drove in the valley where this all took place. On foot, it took many days to go from where they were to Galilee, which was a BIG trip. It was lots of overnight stays and lots of walking. If you were wealthy you got to ride a donkey. So Mary and Joseph went back and where did they find him? They found him sitting with what Christianity calls the Doctors of Law — the Sages. Every year during one of the High Holy Days (during one of the festivals), the Sages — the Wise Men — open up the doors to the temple to anyone who wants to come and discuss and debate the Word of God. Where did they find him? He was sitting with the Sages, just debating away.

First of all, he was just old enough as he had to be of the age of accountability. Young people need to learn this. You may still be covered under your family — true — but you are directly accountable to God. Otherwise he wouldn't have been allowed to discuss with the Sages. Since the discussion seemed to be going on for quite a while, he must have known some stuff! Jesus was not at that time filled with the Spirit. He was walking as a man. Hear what I'm saying. I hear more excuses — "Well Jesus was God." He walked as man. So Mary and Joseph found their son, and He of course said, "I must be about My Father's business." (Luke 2:49)

If you look at what happened from His birth up until the time of His death and resurrection, why did the representation of God on earth have to receive the Holy Spirit? Why did we have to see Him enter in? Why did He have to be baptized by John the Baptizer? Why did the dove come down? Why did we hear about the voice? Because God the Father and God the Son wanted to show how we are able to do the same as Yeshua.

Teaching about the crucifixion of Christ, Matthew 27:46 says, "And about the ninth hour Jesus cried with a loud voice, saying 'Eli, Eli, lama sabachthani?' That is to say, 'My God, My God, why hast thou forsaken me?' " With due respect to the King James Version, this is not the best translation. What Yeshua said was "Father, Father why have you put me in this mess?" or "Why have you turned from me?" Yeshua never said, "Father, Father why have you left me?" Yeshua suffered as man. He was tortured as man. He was supernaturally given that power to resist. Everything that we see Him doing all along is that of an "ensample."

David, when he was in his time of deepest travail, has been quoted as saying the same thing. Not true. He cried out to God, "Eli, Eli, lama azavtani?"(Psalm 22:2, Tanach) David said to God, "My God, My God, why hast thou forsaken me?" (Psalm 22:1, KJV) Today we might say, "Why have you abandoned me?" Yeshua never doubted that the Father was with Him in His suffering, He only questioned the reason for His pain. He did not feel abandoned by God the Father. David, however, is pleading with God to rescue him from his circumstances and does not understand why God has not saved him. We should not be like David.

As we develop as spiritual warriors, we must remember that Yeshua is our ensample, the way we should live. There are times that we do not understand why we are in the mess we are in, and we do — and should — cry out to God. We turn again to Romans 8:28, "And we know that all things work together for good to them that love God, to them who are the called according to His Purpose." This is the message of faith for the trials that God allows.

I have learned over the years — through all the bumps and bruises — that I used to look upon myself as instructed by God, and that He had different levels of instruction. I lived in the two-by-four section! Whenever God needed something from me He'd pick up a two-by-four because I wasn't listening real well. I actually was listening, but I was so busy wanting to do it my way that I'd get whopped upside my head and I'd go "Okay!" I finally got tired of the two-by-fours and I moved to the little sticks, and I moved from the little sticks to the feathers. I moved into the feathers and said, "Okay — let's not do bad things." It wasn't bad things; He was just getting my attention. I have to tell you at no time was this punishment because all God was doing was fulfilling the intent of my heart. God looks at the intent of your heart.

God the Father sent the Messiah as an ensample because this is what people need. He sent Him to save the earth because the way so-called "obedient" people were headed was unto destruction because of disobedience. Look — look closely; look at it physically and look specifically because otherwise you're going to lose the war. God's not waiting for evil to get you. He may wipe us out as with Noah, only this time not with water. He's got lots of other things, and fire I understand. The next stage is we'll all be crispy critters if we don't get it right. But that's not relevant. What's relevant is the Messiah, who had knowledge, walked as man with the power of man.

We saw the fulfilling of the Holy Spirit with the representation of the dove. Then the Lord's voice came out of heaven saying, ". . .This is my beloved Son, in whom I am well pleased." (Matthew 3:17) How would you like to hear "Oh my good and faithful daughter. . .Oh my good and faithful son?" I think it's the most exciting thing I've ever heard! I don't care when, I don't care if it's the last second on earth, and I don't care if it's standing before Him in judgment. We all will stand in judgment. I want God to say to me "My good and faithful son, I am well-pleased with you." What a great reward that would be!

Going back to the Messiah, we watch and see Him and know what we're supposed to do, because now we come back to the spiritual war. We come back to the war between good and evil. I have to watch and learn from childhood what Jesus did, and how He did it. I have to see how He went, how He was empowered and how He empowered His people. How did He empower the disciples? Did he tell them go do this, go do that? Is that what He said? No, He spoke in parables. Job spoke in parables. Job was sitting on the floor with his wife telling him to curse God and die. (Job 2:9) He wouldn't do it, but he kept speaking God's Word.

I know I'm jumping around, but the heroes of the Bible were not heroes because they were strong. No one is strong without God. You can say to me "Oh, you're a pretty big guy. You use to do martial arts; you've been in the military and have done all this shooting and stuff." I used to have an old saying. It's a bit of an Italian saying with a little Jewish mixed in. "Aaaaah!" Hear that? "Aaaaah!" Say this at the same time as you make a quick motion of the entire hand.

Without the absolute power of God, I'd be dead! They told me in 1992 that I was doomed. Get you're things in order—you're through. I had heart trouble, damage to the back of the heart, and degenerative arthritis on my spine and joints so bad that I couldn't pick up ten pounds without screaming. I had no breath, I could barely walk—couldn't walk, actually. I was in pain and in a wheelchair, yet God healed me and I will outlive most of those doctors unless they get saved and healed themselves. I will, because God has promised me, and all I promise God is obedience to the best of my ability.

Let's get back to the intent of the heart. What God did for me was because of His great mercy. He did what He had to do—whatever it took—because He knew the intent of my heart. What is the intent of your heart as you read this book? What is the intent of your heart through whatever you're going through? What is the intent of your heart as you sit there? "I'm a believer. I'm saved." What do you do with it?

I was one of the most dangerous men in the world as far as my training, my education, and what I did for a living. If I had sat home in my living room, no one would have been in any danger. I know people who are professional students. They have knowledge and strings of degrees, but they don't use them. My wife has quite a few degrees and she used them. Now she's using them for the power and direct service to God! God reads the intent of your heart. If you expect God to provide for you, if you expect God to protect you from the evil of this world, you can't be protected in your house. You can't be protected in your living room. You can't be protected even if you go find an island — like I thought about doing before I was a believer. There is nowhere to run, nowhere to hide, yet we as believers need to begin to change this earth.

You need to know who you are, who God is, and know your empowerment. I'm talking about the ability to point your finger in the name of Jesus and take dominion and make physical changes on this earth. I'm talking about the fact that we are the majority. You'll find that over ninety percent of the United States population wants God in their lives. Which God, how God, right God, wrong God, but they want a superior being in their lives. We know it would be preferable that it be the God of Abraham, Isaac and Jacob — Yeshua our Messiah Jesus. We'll let the Holy Spirit deal with that.

I used to be in the hierarchy of the Israeli military, even sitting in general staff meetings. When I was sent out on a mission, I wasn't worried about what the general was doing or who was in charge of me. Just the same as I don't worry about what God is doing. I wasn't worrying about how much support I was getting. I knew if I put my hand behind me there'd be ammunition in my hand. I knew that someone was behind me so that if I got stuck someplace he was going to run up and give me what I needed. I never checked on it. Why? I trusted my command structure! Do you trust yours? When I was a sniper, a whole unit went out ahead of me and they did all the groundwork. They found the target and I got whisked in and they went "There!" I didn't sit there for the next five hours checking it out. I didn't say, "Are you sure?" I didn't say, "Am I safe?" Why? It's because I trained and trusted that I'm alive today. There were a few close calls, but I'm alive because of God.

Do you know what trust is? Do you know what the foundational meaning of trust is? Belief. God said He will keep me and I believe He's a big enough God. Never mind He's proven it to me many times. I believe that He is a big enough God. I believe that if this building starts to collapse — God forbid — at this moment, and I'm not done with my work, I will raise my hand up and cry out to the Messiah. I'm not exactly sure what I'm going to say, but I will cry out to the Messiah, and I will live! And if I die I will rise up out of the ashes and do what I need to do. You know why? Not because

I'm a maniac, but I do it because God said so. You hear that? It's because God said so! In Israel we say, "Hinei kavur ha'kelev," which means, "This is where the dog is buried." In English you might say, "This is the crux of the matter."

The secret is that I believe! I believe God is my active Lord and my active Savior! I believe Him as my commander, my general, my director, my God, my Lord! I believe if He says that I can work in the flames, evil will not triumph over good. I am the representation of good even if I'm not perfect, even if I don't succeed perfectly in pure thoughts each and every day. It's by the power vested in me, not by any state in the world, but by the power of the Holy Spirit and the blood of the sacrifice of our Messiah Yeshua—Jesus.

I believe I will walk as a warrior; where His light in me shines, evil will flee. Where the light shines, the darkness flees. Have you ever heard of the darkness piercing the light? No, never does darkness pierce the light. Darkness is the absence of light, and when light fills the room, darkness leaves. When righteousness and justice walk into the room, evil will flee. Whether it's in prayer, whether it's in intercession, or whether it's just you walking and invoking God in your heart, righteousness will reign. Only empty rooms are owned by the devil; only where the righteous believers do not stand, does the devil reign.

God has made certain promises. Do what you're supposed to, follow God's Word and accept yourself as a soldier in God's army. Believe in the Word, in the one true living God, in the Messiah, in the Holy Ghost and the empowerment of "I am the temple of the Holy Spirit!" Within you is the power to do all that the Messiah has done and even greater things in His name. You will point your finger and take dominion! If you believe these things now is the time to begin doing them!

Chapter 15

JOINING GOD'S ARMY

*G*od is the truth and in that truth is power and life and the implementation of that truth. I am a Warrior of the one true living God. I believe that only through Him and His power will I live and breathe this day. I believe that if I walk out from under the mighty hand of God — to which I have submitted myself — then I will surely die. Submit yourself under the mighty hand of God, and He will exalt you in due time.

As I listen to the Word of God, I should do everything in my power to get the cracks sewed up and get the armor wrapped up thick enough and heavy enough that the devil will not be able to sneak in. The cracks and crevices in my armor are disobedience. The shallow cracks are brought about by disobedience, and the holes in the armor are brought about by unbelief!

There is ongoing and continuing disobedience in many different places where we've given room to the devil. You know I've said this many, many times. Nobody has to guess who I am. Never mind that I walk around with a yarmulke on my head. I can take it off, put on dirty old jeans and walk around in the darkest, nastiest places. When someone talks to me, it doesn't take them long to know who I am. It is as the Lord said to Moses, "I Am, that I Am" (Exodus 3:14). In Hebrew we say, "Ehyeh-Asher-Ehyeh."

I don't care how intellectual you are, how intelligent you are, or how much you think you know. There are many people reading this that know more Bible than I ever will know. The question is what then? Is it a weapon, or a chunk of knowledge that we're doing nothing with? You need to take a stand. The only stand I can tell you is: make sure your armor is correct. Make sure you know the Word of God and make sure that you are actively living the Word of God. You can dig ditches or run major corporations and be in line with God. Believe it or not, you can be an attorney — forgive me all of you out there — and follow God's Word.

The letter of the law does not confine us. We're not wrapped in the chains of it, but let me tell you something; we're not freed from obeying it. You have to remember that Matthew 5:17-18 says "Think not that I am come to destroy the law or the prophets: I am not come to destroy, but to fulfil. For verily I say unto you, Till heaven and earth pass, one jot or one tittle shall in no wise pass from the law, till all be fulfilled." That's what the Lord says to us.

I ask you, do you fit God into your lives? Do you work really hard at fitting God into your lives? Well, you can't. God is too big to fit into your life. God is way too big; you have to fit into God. Everything that you do, everything that you are, everything that you possess, and everything that you judge is judged by God and His Word. Your actions are based on that. Every profession — that is moral and correct — can be based upon the absolute Word of God from Genesis to Revelation. Here comes the question: Will you stand before the Lord or will you kneel before the enemy?

You know that terrorists are trying to hit us all the time. It's only by prayer and intercession, and 18,000 plus law enforcement agencies working together that have stopped more explosions from occurring. What if a bomb goes off? Who's going to bring the light? Who's going to walk in righteousness? It will be a believer who brings God's truth. The believer will not be running into the street saying, "God, why have you forsaken me?" You can understand that this is an attack of evil, and you will be out there helping to pick up people. Tell them, "Fear not! The Lord God of Abraham is with us! Fear not! Jesus is Lord! This is just an attack of the devil. We will reign!"

Unfortunately there are people in the background waiting for these disasters so they can bring compromise. There are national and international organizations waiting to be the ones when darkness comes to bring more darkness. My question is to you when and if this disaster comes, will you stand with the light? Are we going to let FEMA (Federal Emergency Management Agency) take over completely? If there is a major emergency, they have the power over police, army, navy, and every piece of bread, electricity and resource in the entire USA. They will have that control.

If you pick up a newspaper today and you see that there's a lie in it, will you take a few minutes and write a letter to your editor and say that this is a lie? Stand up and say that this is not who God is — this is not what God says. Perhaps someone has been spreading a lie about Israel. Are you going to stand up and be able to say it is a lie? Never be still and never be silent!

The Lord sent me to England with a word in March 2005 to tell them that it's time to stand before the Lord or kneel before the enemy. To be a warrior you have to be willing to give it all up. Now we're not talking only about money here, we're talking about are you willing to give up your pride, your position? What you think is your honor? Are you willing to speak the truth of God to everybody around you? Even to your friends or your family? Everything I'm saying to you is in this Word of God. The Messiah told us He didn't come to make peace, but that He came to separate you from your mother, sister — everyone in the world.

We are talking about a declaration of war. Are you ready? Say "I" (say your name) "I declare that I am a member of God's army. I declare this! I declare that wherever I can see around me right now, I will not tolerate evil." You're not going to go be a policeman and you're not going to scream at people or arrest them. Remember that wherever we see, we have power — much power. Say to yourself, "I (say your name) have much power. I have the power vested in me by the one true living God by His Holy Spirit. And my power is the truth — the truth of the Word of God."

Someone may say, "Well, that's not my truth." You can say, "Well fine then, but not within these ten yards. You can have your truth and I'll have mine as long as you leave me alone and you leave mine alone." I will not be silent. You see, I can't take over the land and neither can you, but if it's my ten yards and your ten yards, that's how revival takes place. Each individual becomes revived and that revival brings light that washes across the world.

I want us to wash across the land. Be pro-active, positive and truthful. Speak the Word of God the best you can. Live the Word of God the best you know how. Learn the Word of God more so you can live the Word of God better. Be the ensample that the Messiah wants us to be, because He lived, died and rose again for us. He suffered so that we can be that ensample on this earth. I'm not talking in a physical sense. Do not allow lies in your ten meters, in your newspaper, in your household, in your place of work. If someone refuses, then don't be their friend. Don't be part of them, but don't throw them out. Be a witness to them, but separate them from your ten meters.

Christians want to say the truth, as we know it. Others can have their so-called truths, but not in my living room, not in my schools. That's what we're learning now. You are a child of God. You are a warrior in the army of God led by Christ. You have the sword of the Lord; you have the power and protection of the Holy Spirit. You have the shield, the breastplate, the loins girded, and the truth upon your feet. (Ephesians 6) Walk into the land and take dominion! Remember this is only the beginning as you will learn and study through the rest of your life.

Pray the Messiah will come soon. As a warrior you are the "Army of One," and that "One" is the truth, and the Word is the truth. Jesus is Lord!

Chapter 16

UNDERSTANDING
WHO YOU ARE

*have always had a very inquisitive mind. When I was a child, I asked the rabbi who the "Us" is when God stated in Genesis 1:26, ". . .Let Us make Man in Our image. . ." I did not understand it until I was saved. The Jewish people who have not yet accepted the Lord do not understand that to this very day. As a matter of fact, I have been yelled at because I'm teaching "multiple gods." Well, I only know this "One" God.

What has this got to do with spiritual warfare? You need to understand who you are, who God is, the rights and powers that you have been blessed with, and your abilities. For example, " . . . ye shall be my sons and daughters, saith the Lord Almighty." (Second Corinthians 6:18) If you accept the Lord, you may become and should become sons and daughters of God—with the power to do the things that He has granted us. If you do not accept God as God and if you do not accept the Messiah as Lord, then you're defenseless because the war is coming. By the time that you hear of attacks somewhere, there will be more attacks somewhere else. Now you ask, "How is that possible?" Remember God gave the devil dominion over the earth except for those who receive the Lord as Savior. The devil has no dominion over those who accept the Bible as our instruction manual and those of us who believe in the one true living God through the Messiah.

Christian pride is a terrible thing. I may know how to talk, I may say good things, but I understand that God gives me grace and that I myself will sound pretty stupid. Sometimes I think that what I'm saying doesn't make any sense whatsoever, but that is when the teaching is usually the best. The Lord tells us to stand before kings and to stand before man. Don't worry what you will say, just trust in the Lord and open your mouth. Let me tell you what you have to start trusting for—everything! Start trusting Him for all things! Today is the war and you are the warriors! Have you ever awakened in the morning and wondered why you're struggling so much? Have you ever wondered why you're having all these attacks? You are at war.

Whether you like it or not, we are Judeo-Christian. I am as Christian as you are and you are as Jewish as I am. The only difference is that you don't have to follow the traditions of the Old Testament unless you wish to. You need to follow the commands of the Old Testament but not the laws. You don't have to follow the chains of the law but as God tells us, the Ten Commandments haven't gone away. You still shall not steal and you still shall not have any God before Him.

It's important to understand that God says in Deuteronomy 5:7, "Thou shalt have none other gods before me." Well, does that mean its okay just because you don't worship Allah, or you don't worship Buddha? One of the things that get in the way of the power of most warriors—or those who want to be warriors—is that if there's anything in your life that you put before God, then that becomes your God. This includes your wife, your husband, your children, your favorite car, your favorite ice cream, or your job. You say to yourself, "But I have to be diligent." Yes, but you are equipped to be diligent at your job with God. You say, "Well what about when I'm forced to work, and I have no time to do God's stuff?" Well if you have no time to do God's stuff then God has no time to do your stuff. We are not to "forsake the assembling of ourselves together." (Hebrews 10:25)

I have found that the meaning of "pray without ceasing" (First Thessalonians 5:17) is to be in communication with God. When I first heard about "pray all the day long," I wondered how I was going to do that. My understanding of prayer—coming from a Jewish home—is that I'm wrapped up in a prayer shawl, I have my prayer book in front of me, I'm bouncing up and down and I'm praying and talking to God. I'm looking up to God, I'm looking down, I'm looking sideways and I'm talking to God. I'm asking Him, "What's going on. . . how do I eat, how do I walk, how do I talk, how do I drive, how do I not stick myself in the cheek with a fork when I'm trying to eat?" Then I came to an understanding as I studied. That's why the Lord requires us to study to show ourselves approved. (Second Timothy 2:15) I realized that prayer is communication.

That may seem very easy for you who have been in Christianity all your life, but at thirty-nine years old I came from of one of the most rigidly framed faiths in the world. You did everything by the numbers and you did it all day long. You had 613 overt acts and prayers that you did all the day long, not counting praying three times a day aside from that. Orthodox Jews are bound by the interpretation of Torah with rules written by the rabbis. They think they have to do all of them or they're going to hell; they won't be written in the Lamb's Book of Life this year. You know it's a difficult thing to try and follow the regiment of 613 commands to do each day. The first command is to thank Him when you wake up in the morning. Then you begin to dress, and as you dress you thank the Lord for the abilities, you thank Him for the clothing. It goes on and on.

However, we know that by accepting the Messiah Yeshua— Jesus—that we are in the Lamb's Book of Life. We are going to heaven! The awareness that God requires—that He asked Abraham for and that He asks us for—is that when we open our eyes in the morning, we are aware of the one true living God. Thank Him for waking you.

These are the things you have to understand to be able to speak as a warrior of Christ, a warrior of David, and a warrior of the Bible. We need to understand what is going on. It's important that we understand the order of things and recognize the teaching the Lord gives us. Prayer is communication with God. It's not the bouncing up and down and doing. That's not the Word of God. Don't sit and read all the time. It's not that. Talk with the Lord God all the day long in everything you do.

Why did God create us? What was the purpose? God created us to know that He is God. He created us so that we would recognize Him as God and King. He also created us so He would be able to give us everything that we need. Our job is to know God and to recognize Him. Our job is to make sure God knows that we know His job. Listen to what I just said. Your job, my job is to recognize

God, to know that He is the Lord, to know His promises to me, and to make sure that I let Him know that I know. If I call upon Him and let Him know that I know that I recognize Him, then He will keep me.

As we continue to study the Word of God you say, "But wait, what have I learned? What are you telling me?" I'm telling you that you have to believe in God, I'm telling you that you have to begin to speak the truth. The truth is that the one true living God through the Messiah is the only way. I had the opportunity to be reinstated with my Jewish people and my Jewish nation, but I would not forsake and deny the Messiah. You may not be asked to deny Him, but are you willing to be for Him? Will you be pro-active?

The United States of America is founded on those principles. If you are a worshipper of something else, you have that freedom. Don't tell me its okay; don't tell me that people who are trying to destroy Israel are righteous. Don't tell me that right is wrong, and wrong is right. (People will say that—it's a given—but, you could say something like "You're not going to tell me it's ok and expect me to agree with it.") When you're sitting with a group of your friends or acquaintances and they start talking trash about God or about what's going on in politics, and you know what they're saying is not lining up with the Word of God, will you keep your mouth shut because you're afraid that they won't like you? Are you willing to call the White House and say, "This is ridiculous! How can you force or try to force a nation to make peace with people who are still trying to kill you?"

Are you willing to speak up and declare that I am a member of God's army? As a believer, you have to be willing. We need to learn the Word, we need to speak the Word and we need to sit and pray. However, there is also activism. I'm not telling you to go out and picket, as I'm not even sure I agree with picketing. But there are emails, there are phone calls, there are places around the world that you can reach to tell the truth—not just the truth of salvation, but the active truth of dominion. I'm not saying we need to convert anyone; it is the Word that converts us and the Holy Spirit that brings conversion or fulfillment. This is what we're supposed to be doing.

If the president said something that doesn't line-up with the Word, speak up! I understand he's the president and he's got to consider the whole country; however, if lies are being told, we have the right to take dominion. Every now and then my wife and I will look at an article in the newspaper and the lie is so ridiculous that my wife can't do anything but sit down in front of the computer and put a letter together and send it to the editor. She quotes the truth, and the truth is what wins. Often the lies are about Israel. People ask me, "Why is it wrong to come against Israel?" God said right at the beginning, "Those who bless thee will be blessed, and those who curse thee will be cursed." (Genesis 12:3)

You do not have to submit to lies. The government is of the people (or should be), by the people, and for the people. This country was founded on Judeo-Christian principles. The next time somebody says that there must be separation of church and state, remember it is a lie that some liberal judges are trying to force. What do you mean by church? We had the Ten Commandments first! Moses was a Jew! The Ten Commandments are the foundation of the New Testament, and the Ten Commandments are the foundation of this country. Our forefathers founded a nation where all could be free in their worship, but the government would not make a religion. The First Amendment says that the government of this nation shall not establish a government religion and force others to worship it or forbid public assembly. That's it, and yet you have judges who, instead of judging, are recasting and creating the law. What is right wing, what is left wing? There's only God's Word or the lack thereof.

We should have nothing to fear from this spiritual war. We should have nothing to fear from explosions. I would like to avoid them, as I've been in the middle of some and you don't want to be there. We should not fear the bullets of the enemy, whether they are the evil of sin or whether they are the bullets of a rifle. I would rather avoid both, but the Lord has promised us that He will protect us and that He will keep us. Your requirement is to recognize these promises and to believe in them. You have to believe on the Giver of these promises in order to receive the power of these promises.

Chapter 17

YOUR POSITION
AS A WARRIOR

et me tell you a story. I knew a Christian psychologist who was working with Christians, and I walked up to him one day and half-jokingly said, "Tell me when these people will stop paying your fee? When will they stop needing you as a psychologist? I mean we're all Christians. What do we need to do?" He told me that when they finally realize that Jesus is Lord they wouldn't need him anymore.

I've been giving you specifics on what you need to do to be a soldier in God's army, but it's going to be up to you at some point to make the decisions to say, "YES, I believe that God is God. YES, I believe that the Word is accurate as written. YES, I believe what God told me to do I'm supposed to do, and what He told me not to do; I'm not supposed to do. When I'm not sure of what I'm supposed to do, I won't do because it's easier to do a do you didn't than to undo a don't you did." Now you may have to reread that about six times and figure out what I just said.

I have an advantage because I was brought up Jewish, in an Orthodox home. When I was little, my mom (may she rest in peace) made sure that when I was in her lap that I was warm and happy and fed. She told me I should remember that all the good, all the warmth, all the great and gracious things that are happening are from God through her. I remember her telling me that the Messiah is coming. She never told me about Jesus because we were not a believing household. We were an Orthodox Jewish household. For those of you who don't know, most Jews do not believe that the Messiah has come yet. They surely don't believe that it's Jesus. When I got older and I could be with my dad (and I was allowed to go with him), he always made it clear to me that he was a working person, and the paycheck we got was not from his boss. God allowed his boss to sign it. It was God that did these things.

Do you realize that in the Old Testament times the only way to have the Holy Spirit was to be touched by God as a prophet? God's hand came down directly. Back then, the only way you could receive the Holy Spirit was God would take possession of you and He would speak through you. After you spoke, the Lord was gone and you waited for the next time. A false prophet was put to death because it meant God was not speaking through him. Many of today's prophets speak for themselves. I never wanted to sense the full power of God and then have Him leave.

When I became a believer and received the fullness of God, I realized that I am the temple of the Holy Spirit, and that God is residing in me all the time. What great power and what great fullness! If you aren't sensing that, you are wasting your time and your energy. It's the greatest high of your entire lifetime to know that you possess the Holy Spirit. Now you sit out there and you say to yourself "Well, I've never had that sense—I've not heard. People say that God talks to them but I've never had God talk to me." My question to you is "Are you listening? Have you invited Him? Have you assumed the position?"

When I was a sniper instructor I would yell, "Assume the position!" Everybody knew what position to get in because we spent months teaching them the kneeling position, the standing position, the prone position, the off-hand position for pistols. I didn't have to tell them to "Do thus and so and thus and so." That's how we get into position. We need to study the Word of God so when you hear "assume the position" you know what it is.

I know that I know that I am a child of God. I know that I know that I am a warrior of David. I know that I know that I stand in God's army and that the Messiah brought me into that. I know that. Why? It's because the Bible tells me so. You know the child's song "The Bible Tells Me So?" I know it because it says so. I recognize that as absolute accuracy because of my position in God. Some say, "Are you some kind of dummy? You take God's word at verbatim?" Yep!

Belief in God is not an intellectual thing that we need to study, learn and accept in our minds. Our minds are what we use to learn what God says we're supposed to do. You have to accept God because He is God — He has to be your position.

Let me give you an example. The Hebrew faith is one of the most rigid, prayer-bound and locked-in religions. When I would start to do my prayers I could tell you where I'd start and 21 ½ minutes from now I'm going to be bowing three times facing that way. I always remembered the ending and stepping backwards. I could tell you exactly every time that's where I was going to wind up because that's the way it was. You may have heard about the 613 commandments that a Jewish man should follow from morning till night. A father who wanted his son to be a better follower of the Bible codified the instructions — what he thought a good Jewish boy should do to become a good Jewish man, a follower of the one true living God. Jewish authorities had the power to say, "This is what all the Jews in the world are going to do today." That's where this came from.

When I accepted the Messiah, I became a Christian. I didn't know anything about Messianic Judaism. I knew the Messiah was named Jesus, and that there was a whole other section of the Bible I needed to learn. Christians, on the other hand, were another question. There were many, many things in Christianity and the churches that to my mind were like "Oh boy, I don't know about this." But you know what? I did them anyway until I could figure out what was the doctrine of Christ and what was dogma of man. But I did it first. I didn't wait until I understood and I was sure it was intellectually correct. I did it because I believed that God said so.

If there is dogma (something God didn't command in His Word), it's up to me whether I want to do it or not. In our Messianic congregation, we are not rabbinical. What does that mean? There are congregations that require their members to follow what the rabbis prescribe. However, it is impossible to do each and every rabbinical requirement in perfection. That's why there is the grace and mercy of the Lord. We are freed from the chains but we are not freed from the commands of God. We, as a Biblical congregation, obey what's in the Bible.

What is my stand? What is my position? My position is that I am a child of the Lord, I believe in His word as accurate, I will follow His Word to the best of my knowledge, and I will expound and expand my knowledge the best I can in every day and in every way. One of the things He says in that knowledge is that I should submit. What do I submit to? My pastor? I submit to him only if he's telling me the Word of God. I don't want you to think you need to rebel against your pastor tomorrow if he makes a mistake. Let's not do that. But we need to be positioned and in submission to the Word of God. We are getting into the nitty-gritty of the positions we need to assume to be a true warrior.

What am I submitting to? If it's not in the Word of God, I'm not going to do it. If I receive instructions from someone to do something that goes against the Word of God, no matter what the cost — I'm not going to do it. I'm also not going to break God's law, which says, ". . .Render therefore unto Caesar the things which are Caesar's; and unto God the things that are God's." (Matthew 22:21) I'm not going to break a democratic law, but if they outlawed the Bible tomorrow in the United States, I'd be an outlaw. If the law says I'm not allowed to put the Ten Commandments in the city square, I won't put it there. I will become those Ten Commandments. I will speak them; I will do them because that's what we're talking about — being warriors. If they outlawed being a believer — if they outlawed carrying a Bible, then I'm not going to stop.

We don't have to worry about that today. We're losing the war without them declaring it! You understand that? Islam believes that we are a thin-blooded, democratic, free nation who follows the Judeo-Christian God, and we are absolute wimps as far as they're concerned. They believe our God is a wimp because of the way we act. They believe that if they strike us hard enough, knock us over, kill enough innocent men, women and children, and disrupt our comfortable way of life, they will force our government to accept their way of life.

When Al-Qaeda hit the towers on 9-11, the first demand was to "get out of the Middle east," then a couple of weeks later the demand was to "Convert to Islam." My position is if you want to be Islamic, be Islamic but leave me alone. You cannot force me; you will not force me because my God is the powerful God. My God is the God of truth and my God is the God of love. Love means I don't lie.

My wife and I agree that if the Messiah would come tomorrow. . . bye, we're out of here, see you. Until then my wife knows she's number two in my life. She comes before my ministry, but after God, and it's the same with her. I am number two after God. The reason we get along so well is because our right and wrong is based upon the Word of God. We disagree on many things from time to time, and our choosing is that we wish to please God rather than one another. We find out that if we please God, then we please one another in the long run. We had to do that by submitting. Yes she submits to me but I also submit to her through the Word of God. Christ spread His arms and died for us! The Word tells me that I am supposed to care for my wife as Jesus cared for the church. Am I supposed to spread my arms and die? I'm willing to try and do that if necessary, but what I have to do is live the way Christ lived.

How does position and submission—my position as a child of God and my submission to God—how does that generate faith? What is faith? "Now faith is the substance of things hoped for, the evidence of things not seen." (Hebrews 11:1) My idea of faith is believing. For example, if I tell you I'm going to pay your bills, and if I show up on the first of the month and pay your bills then you have faith that I will pay your bills. It means you believe.

If you understand your position, if you understand that you are submitted to the Word of God and you're doing it to the best of your ability, it's because you have faith in Him. If you believe that God is your provision, that He is your keeper, that He makes and keeps you healthy; if you believe that the air you breathe is not by coincidence and that He makes your lungs work on a minute by minute basis—how can you disobey?

I believe that if I went into full disobedience—unrepentant dis-obedience—I would drop dead. I don't think anyone in the world can keep me alive today except the one true living God, because doctors think I'm a walking miracle. I belong to a large club of believers we call "The Should-a-been Dead Club." We did not die because of the power and might of God, and we are warriors today.

A warrior's declaration is that I will not allow evil to speak in front of me and I will speak only the Word of God. I will have only the mind of Christ. I will do these things within the ten yards that I have around me. I will not allow untruth—no matter what the cost. You are a warrior of the one true living God if you declare so. If you are in the position of faith, if you are in submission to God, and if you have generated faith, trust and belief in the one true living God, then you are a Warrior in Him.

Chapter 18

PROTECTED UNDER
THE HAND OF GOD

"*H*umble yourselves therefore under the mighty hand of God, that He may exalt you (lift you up) in due time." (First Peter 5:6) Exalting you is way more than lifting you. God's hand should be over the believer, but through disobedience God lifts His hand. Why is that? God doesn't leave you or forsake you. God doesn't smite you. He allows things to happen, but He doesn't cause them. He doesn't have to, because there's evil poised around the whole world to attack you, whether you like it or not.

If you have accepted the Messiah, if you have accepted the Lord, you are a member of God's army. For those of you who have not accepted the Lord, if you're saying to yourself, "Oh good, I'm not in God's army so I'm not a target." No—you're worse! You're cannon fodder for the devil, because if you're not serving God, you are serving the devil. "How can you say that, Rabbi?" Well, the Bible says it. "So then because thou art lukewarm, and neither cold nor hot, I will spew thee out of my mouth." (Revelation 3:16)

There is no middle. It's like a very sharp-pitched roof. You can't stand on the middle or you will slip down and hurt yourself. You're either on God's side or you're on the devil's side. "But I never do anything wrong—I never do anything." If you are not actively seeking the Word of God and actively trying to do that which God has commanded you this day, then you are in the devil's service, and when he's finished with you, he will chew you up and spit you out. If you've not accepted the Lord, now would be a great time. It is a prerequisite to having the power of God. It is a requirement to be able to serve as an active member.

You know there is a rear guard in the military. When I was serving in the Marine Corps, or when I was a sniper, we went to the front, we got shot at and shot back, and then we had a place we could go back to and rest without any need to be on the alert. Then I went undercover, and there was no rear position. There was no fully safe place and I always had to be ready, even when I was in my own home, or even when I was in the shower. I always had a weapon handy where I could reach it.

The difference today is—as a warrior of the one true living God—I am always safe. I am safe wherever I am, if I have on the armor of God. The difference is I don't have to put a pistol in a waterproof bag in the shower where I can get to it. I have the Word of God, I have the sword of the Lord, and angels surround me. I can point my finger at the enemy of the Lord and speak the Word of the Messiah. The devil will lose.

People tell me that I speak openly about Islam and the history of Islam. It's the truth. People say to me, "Aren't you afraid they're going to hurt you?" What can they do to me? Listen—I want to live a very long life. I have a bride and I want to spend time with her until the Messiah comes, or at least 120 years. The Lord has promised me length of days and strength of days. That's where we come to our submission, our position, and our generation of faith. I believe God when He says I can live to 120. I believe God when He says that He will heal me from all things. I believe the one true living God when He says if I stand upon His Word that He will protect me.

Do you believe that if the building starts falling or crumbling down, you can reach your hand up and cry out to the Lord? All you have to do is say "Jesus!" If your time on earth is not done and God has things for you to do, do you believe that you will rise up out of the rubble? I do! Can I die? Yes! It has to be God's will. Can I be martyred? Anytime! But I have survived things that are not survivable.

How are we to get God's hand back upon us? I had a word for England in 2005. I told them to stand before the Lord or kneel before the enemy. You have to get in position, you have to be submitted to the Word of God, and you have to have the level of generated faith that you believe that if the building falls you will survive. If God said something in the Word is going to happen, it will happen. You cannot prevent God's will. The Lord said there would be "great tribulation" upon the earth. (Matthew 24:21) My word to England was "There will be disaster, but will you be the light in that darkness of the disaster? Will you begin to turn from the evil and begin to turn back to God? In turning back to God, will you become that warrior?"

There was a woman in London who led a great intercessory prayer ministry. She was devastated by the word I gave. She and her group believed that if they prayed hard enough God's prophecy would not be fulfilled. This is not a prophecy of the devil. This is not the devil saying these things are going to happen. God said there would be tribulation, God said the remnant will stand and we will be the light of the world. I believe (this is not the Bible — this is a "Moshe"-ism) there will be a bigger remnant than most people think. I do believe that there will be many disasters and many will die. You can't prevent it, but — I use a very fancy word here — you can mitigate it.

After the first set of explosions in London on 7-7 in 2005, I received many phone calls because the prophecy I had spoken had just come true. There were fifty-four dead — which is terrible. What should have happened with four ten-pound bombs of plastic explosives? (A normal bomb in the United States used to be four ounces. You know those big bomb trucks in New York City, with these bomb squads in these big vests? They were carrying three and four ounce bombs, equivalent to two sticks of dynamite, but we're talking about a ten-pound bomb here!) It was a miracle that more people didn't die. The roof of the bus in London blew off with people sitting in the seats! The people in the seats weren't killed! Over seven hundred people were wounded in the attacks. Some were walking around in the explosion area with their clothes completely blown off and not wounded. That's God! Many believe it was a miracle! I'm only one person but I told to people who told people who told people — and that's your job too. It's not to just read this book, but to wrap your mind around it and teach other people.

The intercessors in England had prayed, and they prayed for God's will. Prayer is the war, but doing goes along with it. The Bible (Ephesians 2:8) says very clearly that you're saved by grace through faith—not by works. Faith without works is dead! (James 2:17) Go argue with God if you don't believe what I just said. What the intercessors began to do is declare themselves as warriors and speak the truth. They began to worry not for their own honor, not for their own position, not for their own paycheck, but they began to speak the Word of God. They believed the Word of God, and the hand of God began to return.

How far it's returned—what's going to happen next? We know there was another set of explosions and the bombs didn't go off, only the detonators went off. This is going on all over the world. You can pick up a newspaper—it's not just London. We, as warriors, can take dominion and mitigate the destructions that are coming, not to survive, but to be the light of the world. That's that we are supposed to be. Through our obedience, we bring the mighty hand of God back upon us.

I used to be a hot-rodder. I still am, I just don't speed anymore. I always sped until I had a vision and it was about the hand of God. I again read that powerful Scripture: "Humble yourselves therefore under the mighty hand of God, that He may exalt you in due time." (First Peter 5:6) The mighty hand of the Lord—imagine it! So, here's me and here's God's hand over me. The Word says to obey Caesar, right? (Matthew 22:21) Say the speed limit happens to be 65 mph. Here's God doing 65 mph and here's me doing 75 mph. God doesn't exceed the speed limit, so I drive out from under God's hand when I speed.

That may sound funny to you, but I always wondered why powerful believers had car accidents. I know of one leader who was killed in a car accident. (This was when I was working on this theory of maybe we're doing something wrong.) I believe that this was a man of God. He believed in God, he lived God. I didn't know any other part of his life that wasn't his best attempt to do God's Word. The first thing I wondered was if he had been speeding. He had been.

Humble yourself under the mighty hand of God so He can exalt you in due time! As I was shown, we have God's hand over us, and just like He didn't leave His Son in His tribulation on the cross, He hasn't left us. He lifts up His hand when we are in disobedience. God does not turn from us. God did not turn from Jesus on the cross. If you submit to the Word of God, fully and accurately, have faith He will protect you. Speak out with great expectations that the miracles will come upon you and that the Word of God will give you the strength to do what you need to do. He in His way, in His word, will make You His light, and many will be saved and brought to the Lord!

Chapter 19

A WEAPON FOR TODAY

*ave you ever wondered why the Hebrews wandered for 40 years in the desert and were only attacked once? They had—and we have today—a powerful weapon in the book of Numbers in the Bible. The Lord has given us power to both defend ourselves and to move in the world under the covering of the one true living God. Wandering the desert at night, the Hebrews followed the Lord's flame; during the day they followed the Lord's cloud. When the people of Israel set off in the morning, Scripture says: "And the cloud of the Lord was upon them by day, when they were out of the camp. And it came to pass, when the Ark set forward, that Moses said, 'Rise up, Lord, and let thine enemies be scattered; and them that hate thee flee before thee." (Numbers 10:34-35)

It's no coincidence that the cloud or the flame was ahead of the moving tribe. If you've ever been on a large boat, you'll find that close to the rear of the boat, when it's moving through the water, whether it's calm or very rough, the water behind the boat is calm. This is what happened with Moses and 2 ½ million people. The people always followed behind the cloud or flame for the Lord's protection.

The enemies of God are not trying to attack you; they're after the Lord that resides in you by His Holy Spirit! Therefore if you are closely following God, He battles His enemy and defends you. As long as the Hebrews followed God according to His instructions, the enemies were defeated. This biblical principle has not changed—your life is protected! What good is a bodyguard if he's not with you guarding your body?

At the end of the day, or when the Lord told them it is time to stop, as the ark rested and Moses would say, ". . .Return, O Lord, unto the many thousands of Israel." (Numbers 10:36) Most translations from the Hebrew use "return" as does the King James Version. When I read the Stone Edition of the Tanach, I realized that the meaning was far greater. The Scripture is better translated as, ". . .Reside tranquilly, O, Hashem, among the myriad thousands of Israel." (Stone Edition Tanach)

Jewish synagogues and Messianic Jewish congregations have a cabinet representing the Ark to store the Torah scroll. When the scroll is removed from the Ark, Scripture from Numbers 10:35 is always recited: "And it came to pass when the Ark set forward, that Moses said, 'Rise up, from upon us O Lord, and let thine enemies be scattered; and let those that hate thee flee before thee." When the scroll is returned to the Ark, all recite: "And when it rested, he would say, Return, O Lord, unto the many thousands of Israel."

For years I had visualized that when Moses called upon God, God Himself returned and would hover over the 2 ½ million Israelites. But that's not what it says. It says He "resided tranquilly" among them. The meaning of reside is to "live within." So there's no way we could not be resting tranquilly! I had been a believer in Yeshua for many years before I realized that this Scripture is a foretelling of the Holy Spirit that we have within us. After the Holy Spirit revealed this to me, I have been teaching the meaning of this Scripture. I had never heard this taught in this way and I have been excited to share this prayer with others.

At this point we have to remember that our Lord God through Yeshua—Jesus—said in John 14:12 that "He. . .that believeth on me, the works that I do shall he do also, and greater works than these shall he do; because I go unto my Father." We shall have authority to do all the things that He did in His name, and even those things greater than Him, for we also have dominion over those things not yet seen. The Lord was very specific In His instruction that we had His power by our faith and belief in Him.

John 1:1 says, "In the beginning was the Word, and the Word was with God, and the Word was God." Therefore you must know that you and I have the same authority as Moses to send God forth to protect us just as he did because the same enemy is out there — it hasn't changed — it's still the same devil and his minions.

Whenever you leave your home in the morning, or when you get in your car, turn to the Lord and say, "Rise up from upon me O Lord, and let your enemies be scattered; and let those that hate you flee before you. And out of me shall come forth the Word of the Lord." When you return home at night or wherever you will be staying, take dominion by saying, "Lord I am now resting. Return O Lord and rest tranquilly within me, upon me, for my protection from those that hate you."

This is the same prayer that Moses used, and we may use it at anytime! My bride and I have found when we invoke that prayer it has the same power as it did for Moses in the desert. Why do we want to do this today? It's because God put it in the Bible as a weapon. The Word of God is still the same today as it was yesterday, and the day before, now and forever! I have printed the Scriptures out on cards that we have laminated and given to people. Feel free to photocopy the Numbers prayers, and carry them with you.

"The cloud of the Lord was upon them by day, when they went out of the camp. And it came to pass, when the ark set forward, that Moses said, Rise up, Lord, and let thine enemies be scattered; and let them that hate thee flee before thee. And when it rested, he said, Return, (Reside tranquilly) O Lord, unto the many thousands of Israel."
Numbers 10:34-36   King James Version

> 1) And it comes that when I set forward, I will say to the Lord, "Rise up from upon me, O Lord. Go forth and let thine enemies be scattered. And Let those who hate you flee before you."
>
> 2) And it comes that when I rest, I will say to the Lord, "Lord, I am now rested, and I say to You, Return O Lord and rest tranquilly upon me for my protection from those that hate You."

The one time that the Hebrews were attacked, it was to teach them that they must work together. You can read about it in Exodus 17:8-13. Here's a short version. At the very beginning of their journey they had to show "Achedut" — Hebrew for unity — when they had to work together. What did they discover in that war? When Moses stood representing God with His arms up in the air, they were winning. But when Moses (Moshe in Hebrew) got tired he put his arms down, the Israelites started losing. Moses unto himself did not have power. So they realized that they had to keep Moses' arms up. It required a joint effort.

What was God teaching here? All of us must work together; no one can do it alone. God intends for us to support each other, both physically and spiritually. This is a lesson that Yeshua the Messiah expressed throughout his teaching.

Chapter 20

THE SPIRITUAL WAR

*W*e are now coming to what I call "the wrap" on this book. It doesn't mean the teaching is over. Learning the Word of God in your life and in my life never ends. This is the time for all good men and women to realize that if they are believers in the one true living God, then they are in God's army. Whether you like it or not, you are already in God's army — it's time for you to get on with the war. That may sound harsh to you.

Some people say, "Jesus is God, He's the Messiah, and He is love!" Yes, but the Lord says that we war against principalities of darkness in high places. (Ephesians 6:12) The war is in the heavenlies, but it also says that we have to stand and pray and bring the truth. Every time we bring a believer into the kingdom the angels rejoice! If you study the different translations of the Bible, you will see that many things are clearer than you think! There is a war between good and evil.

Today one evil happens to be Islam. Before it was Hitler, before that it was Greece and all the different nations of the world that were out to destroy God's people. If every Jew disappeared off the face of the earth today, they'd start killing Christians. They do it all over the world! This is an absolute war for survival. It is not just in the flesh, but primarily spiritual. The physical war would stop tomorrow if we won spiritually.

This is a war between Islam (the devil) and God. It is so they can overcome the people of the Book and make them submit.

They look at the way we, as a society, act and they think that our God is a thin-blooded God because He doesn't destroy us. Well, if nothing else, they are dedicated. The Wahhabi sect is the most fundamental, therefore violent, bloodthirsty sect of Islam. They have over 30,000 mosques and schools around the world that are financed by Saudi Arabia.

When terrorists try to destroy Israel, it's not only because they wanted to see this little state go away or they just wanted to kill people called Hebrews. They were trying to kill the people who they call are keepers of the Book. They are trying to kill us today because Judeo-Christians, Christians and Jews are all keepers of the Book. Islam is out to destroy our way of life, our democracy, our freedoms and our faith in the Word of God. There are many denominations in Christianity now saying that Allah is the same God as the God of Abraham. If you have heard this, you've been told a lie.

Mohammed tried to make the Jews on the Arabian Peninsula believe that Mohammed was the Messiah; the first part of the Koran is all loving, kindness, and blessing. That is not a lie; this is a fact, as the Koran says. Then Mohammed went to Medina, but the Jews said, (translated into Brooklynese) "You know what, Bubbella? You ain't no Messiah! You're not our Messiah." You know what? They said the same thing to Jesus, so surely they said it to this guy.

Look in the Koran and see the instructions from Mohammed, which say it's time to kill all the Jews. It says it clearly and it is not a misinterpretation or a misunderstanding. We have read it in Arabic and we have read it in English. You can find translations of the Koran on the Internet. I have challenged Islamic leaders to come and discuss this. They haven't because they can't hide behind the lies when you read their own book to them.

Why am I telling you this? Are you supposed to hate Muslims? No. Are you supposed to hate the evil? Yes. Are you supposed to pray for Muslims? Yes. What are you supposed to pray for? You're supposed to pray for their salvation. Pray that they will find the Messiah. If they won't find the Messiah, pray that they will find and take dominion over a faith that is a faith of death, because there are parts of it that they can bring into life, but there is no God involved. I don't know what we're supposed to do where Islam is concerned, except pray. I was at a broadcaster's convention and Benny Ayalon, who was at that time Israel's Minister of Tourism, stood in front of 7000 people and said, "Why don't you guys convert all the Muslims to Christianity so they'll stop trying to kill us?" You know, he wasn't joking!

I'm not telling to you to try to convert Muslims, but your actions, your life-style should bring people into the Lord. Lifestyle evangelism is one of the most powerful weapons in the world. You can talk about Christianity all you like, you can talk about Messianic-Judaism all you like, but the main problem is with Islam. They look upon us and they see a wimpy God, because they can't understand a God who would put up with us. They believe their Allah would destroy them if they acted this way. That's why they kill each other all the time. They just don't kill us, but they kill anyone who doesn't agree with their way of life.

There are many Muslims who would like peace, but understand that their Koran commands them to kill anyone who will not convert. I'm not telling you to convince your government to go bomb anyone, or take swords out and start flailing about, but Muslims will! What we have to do is take dominion spiritually and physically. What does that mean? It means to join God's army and actively be the light of the world. Remember that God created us as an army. It says it all through the Bible, and He says you don't have to be concerned.

In Exodus 14:15-16 (Tanach) the Lord said to Moses, ". . .Why do you cry out to Me? Speak to the Children of Israel and let them journey forth! And you — lift up your staff and stretch out your arm over the sea and split it. . ." Then He split the sea so that the Hebrews could get away from the Egyptians and then He destroyed the Egyptians. But look at what He said before that in Exodus 14:14, "Hashem shall make war for you, and you shall remain silent." Hello! The King James Version tells us to "be still." Where are you still? We've talked about it before — you need to be in the position. I can only be still in my submission to God when I put my trust and my faith in Him. To be still - you must have heard the saying — let go and let God. Right? How do you let go and let God? You be silent and listen to God.

It's up to us as believers to use the weapons of the Word in prayer and in truth. I'll give you an example. Sometimes I hear someone near me say "God d — it!" I will turn around — even if I don't know this person from Adam — and say, "Excuse me. I promise you that God did not damn it." That's a small thing. If I'm checking out and the person on the register says, "How are you today?" I'll say, "I'm blessed!" Often they look at me and say, "I wish I was." Then of course I can tell them how they can be blessed!

You must declare, "I am a Warrior of the one true living God through Jesus Christ. I will not allow untruth in the area around me." I'm not a policeman and I'm not going to arrest people, but if I hear an untruth I won't shut up. Nobody is going to be allowed to say anything is okay that is not okay with God. I'm sorry- it's costly! We need to stand upon His truths. The United States of America was founded on Judeo-Christian principles for a sole purpose of having a free land under God, indivisible, inseparable, with liberty and justice for all. Sounds corny, but that's the purpose.

The Left, whether in England or the United States, is absolutely seditious, or they're playing stupid. They really believe that you can put your arms around a person who is committed and dedicated by his god to kill you, and your love will convince him to leave you alone. No. You can love them in the Lord; you can show them the salvation of the Messiah, but only through the truth of the Word. Allah is not God; he's their god. Someone who supported the Palestinians once asked, "How can you support Israel so openly?" I told this man truth. He'd never met a Palestinian, he'd never read their doctrine, he'd never read the Koran, and he'd never had any involvement. By the time I finished talking to him, he agreed that he did not know much. I planted a seed in this man's mind; he just didn't know the truth.

When I first met my bride — before she was my bride — she was a member of the "elite Left." She used to think that Palestine is a poor defeated under-dog, Muslims are peaceful, and Israel just wants to take over. She came up to me one day when I told the truth about the Koran, and said "That's not true." I replied, "You are a professional researcher, go research it and prove me wrong." She came back about two weeks later and said "I'm wrong — you're right." You need to seek the Word of God, and if you know the Word of God, you need to speak it. This was a member of my congregation. I had no intention of marrying her, and I could have alienated her completely. She could have walked out. However, I am obligated by my declaration of being a member of God's army to speak the truth.

Unfortunately there are pastors who will not tell the truth because they are afraid of alienating their congregation. I'm not talking about being obnoxious. You can tell the truth without standing up in someone's face. If someone tells you something that you know is not the truth, I don't care if it costs you your job, your honor, or your standing in the community, call them on it. Let me tell you something — I'd rather have right standing before God than have standing in my community. If there are churches that wish to embrace sin, let them embrace sin, but don't call it right. "For the time will come when they will not endure sound doctrine; but after their own lusts shall they heap to themselves teachers, having itching ears." (Second Timothy 4:3) Isaiah 5:20 states, "Woe unto those who speak of evil as good, and good evil. . ."

We are talking about how to stand as a believer in strength, submitted to the Word of God, and walking in faith and belief that God will protect us from all tribulation. We'll have problems, we'll be sick, we'll be attacked, but we'll continue. When my wife is sick I know she is in God's hands. God is God, and I trust God with my wife in His hands. I can tell you that in the flesh I would have reasons not to trust, but I trust Him because His Word says that He is our keeper. Actively declare God's Word, so God's hand will stay above you.

The Word of God says homosexuality is an abomination. Can a homosexual come to my congregation? Yes. Can he sit there and pray with us? Yes. Can he declare that their homosexuality is correct? No. Will they ever be able to tell me they are actively homosexuals and it's okay? No, it's not. I've never asked anyone except one drunk who wouldn't be quiet to step outside — ever! Anyone is welcome in our congregation, but they won't stay there if they don't believe in the Lord. They will come under conviction because we tell the truth. We don't beat up on people, just their actions. I know Christian people who are homosexual and who are celibate. Heterosexuals who are not married should not put themselves in a position of temptation. They should be celibate. You can obey God's Word in every area. If God says "No," it is "No," and you have to say "No." If God says, "Yes," it is "Yes."

You cannot be given the dominion over the earth that God gave us unless you believe. Don't ever forget this, Warrior! God commanded us to take dominion and subdue. Bring the world into the love of God — no longer with guns, knives and swords, but by your faith. Stand by the words out of your mouth and by the confessions that you make that Jesus is Lord. There is no other way.

What you've read in this book is very basic. Do these things and stand upon the truth of the Word, and do not compromise – submit under that mighty hand of God. Speak the Word of the Lord. Live the Word of the Lord in your workday and in your homes, as mothers, fathers, sons and daughters. Everywhere you go you can glorify the word of God, and in that glory comes power! In the heavenlies the angels will defeat evil; it's the truth and it is as supernatural as you can get. These words are powerful, they are mighty because they're simply God, and they are simply the truth.

Have you accepted the Lord as your Savior? Because if you have not, now is the time. All you have to do is say "Come, Lord Jesus." If you're not saved, take the time now if you've never invited the Lord to come into you're life. I don't care what you think you are. I don't care if you say I'm not a Christian, or I'm not a Catholic, or I am a Catholic and I'm not a Protestant. Or I am this, or I am that – it is not relevant. What IS relevant is "Are you a child of God?" If you're not sure, or if you have committed a sin that you have not asked forgiveness for, then this is the time. Take a moment and say to the Lord, "I'm sorry for what I've done, if it's not pleasing to You. Forgive me." He's already died for our sins. You know the forgiveness is already there, you don't have to go seek it out. You just need to say to God, "Hey" – and He'll answer!" He won't be insulted. You can ask Him and say, "Lord, I really messed it up, and I just want it better. I'm tired of being tired." Say to Him, "Come, come to me. I invite you to be my Lord, to be my Savior."

Even if you don't exactly understand yet what that is, agree to agree that He will be your Lord and He will be your Savior. Invite Him to come into your life, and let Him show you what the real power and might of God is. If you haven't done that, now is the time. If you are still in unbelief, decide today if you are a child of God. How do I know if I'm a child of God? Simply believe that God is God and He created the heavens and the earth, and that He created you! He just didn't go poof and put the air around the earth and the atmosphere and hang the planets up there and then say okay, try not to destroy yourselves, and then maybe I'll help a little bit. No! God created us, He gives us every breath and He causes us to live and breathe in Him – now!

God is watching, judging, making, and doing everything in every way. That's what you have to believe. Actually, you don't have to believe anything – but if you want to be a warrior who has some control over your life, who can defeat evil and who can take dominion over the earth as He commanded us to do, then you need to know that God is God. You need to know that the Messiah is Lord and that He did die for us.

All the rest of the things that we said are true, and just remember that the Messiah is the Lord, God is God the Father, God the Son and God the Holy Spirit. The Word is our instruction manual and if we follow it to the fullest, if we do not compromise in this Word, then we will win and we will not go into the darkness. There will be disasters in this country, and we can stand and be the light within those disasters. Do not forget that what you've read here is in the Word. I have said nothing that is not founded and based upon the Word of God. The Word is the Lord and the Lord is the Word, and the Word is the truth, and the truth will fully and completely set you free! Amen!

ENDNOTES

[1]An explanation is required for those who are not familiar with the Tanach, which uses the Hebrew word Hashem, which means "The Name," in the English translation. Hashem is used because the Jewish people never speak the name of God except in prayer. In the Hebrew text, God's name is written with the first four letters of a sentence, YHWH (yud-hey-vav-hey) representing "He was, He is, and He will be." In prayer, YHWH is never pronounced, and "Adoni" is used. The English word is "Lord." Many Christian Bibles use "Lord" in place of Hashem, although some Christians pronounce the Hebrew as "Yah-wey" or "Jehovah."

INDEX

This index is provided as a guide to Hebrew words and phrases spelled phonetically in the text.

Achedut, (אחדות), unity, 92

Adoni, (אדוני), Lord, 101

Baruch Ata Adoni, (ברוך אתה אדוני), Blessed are You, O Lord, iii

Chazak Ve Amatz Em Chochma, (חזק ואמיץ עם חכמה),
   Strong and Courageous with Wisdom, vi

"Ehyeh Asher Ehyeh, " (אהיה אשר אהיה), I Am that I Am," 68

"Eli, Eli, lama azavtani?" (אלי אלי למה עזבתני), "My God, My God, why have you forsaken me?) 62

"Eli, Eli, lama sabachthani?" (אלי אלי למה שבקתנ) "My God, My God, why have you turned from me?" 62

Eshet chayil, (אשת חייל), warrior wife, 57

Hashem, (השם), The Name, 27, 90, 95, 101

Hashkiveinu, (השכיבנו) prostrate yourself before the Lord, 32

Hinei kavur ha'kelev, (הנני קבור הכלב) "This is where the dog is buried." In English, "This is the crux of the matter," 66

Lishmoa, (לשמוע), Listen, hear, obey, 27

Moshe, (משה), Moses, 92

Shalom, (שלום), peace, used for both hello and goodbye, 9

Shofar, (שופר), ram's horn, iii, 33

Tanach, (תנייך), the Hebrew Bible (Old Testament), v, 12, 13, 27, 52, 57, 62, 90, 95, 101

Tzva'ot, (צבאות), hosts, legions or armies, 52

Tzva HaHagana LeYisra'el, (צבא הגנה לישראל), Israel Defense Forces, 52

Torah, (תורה), the five books of Moses, 73, 90

Yeshua, (ישועה) Jesus, 9, 10, 14, 25, 48, 51, 55, 56, 61, 62, 63, 65, 73, 90, 92

Yeshiva, (הישיבה), Hebrew academy, v

Yud-hey-vav-hey, (יהוה), YHWH, the four-letter name of God, representing the first letters of a sentence for "He was, He is, and He will be" 101

CPSIA information can be obtained at www.ICGtesting.com
Printed in the USA
LVOW080521290613

340767LV00004BA/9/P